LIQUIDATION WORLD

SHORT CIRCUITS

Mladen Dolar, Alenka Zupančič, and Slavoj Žižek, editors

The Puppet and the Dwarf: The Perverse Core of Christianity, by Slavoj Žižek

The Shortest Shadow: Nietzsche's Philosophy of the Two, by Alenka Zupančič

Is Oedipus Online? Siting Freud after Freud, by Jerry Aline Flieger

Interrogation Machine: Laibach and NSK, by Alexei Monroe

The Parallax View, by Slavoj Žižek

A Voice and Nothing More, by Mladen Dolar

Subjectivity and Otherness: A Philosophical Reading of Lacan, by Lorenzo Chiesa

The Odd One In: On Comedy, by Alenka Zupančič

The Monstrosity of Christ: Paradox or Dialectic?, by Slavoj Žižek and John Milbank, edited by Creston Davis

Interface Fantasy: A Lacanian Cyborg Ontology, by André Nusselder

Lacan at the Scene, by Henry Bond

Laughter: Notes on a Passion, by Anca Parvulescu

All for Nothing: Hamlet's Negativity, by Andrew Cutrofello

The Trouble with Pleasure: Deleuze and Psychoanalysis, by Aaron Schuster

The Not-Two: Logic and God in Lacan, by Lorenzo Chiesa

What Is Sex?, by Alenka Zupančič

Liquidation World: On the Art of Living Absently, by Alexi Kukuljevic

LIQUIDATION WORLD

ON THE ART OF LIVING ABSENTLY

Alexi Kukuljevic

THE MIT PRESS CAMBRIDGE, MASSACHUSETTS LONDON, ENGLAND

This book was set in Copperplate Gothic Std and Joanna MT Pro by Toppan Best-set Premedia Limited.

Library of Congress Cataloging-in-Publication Data is available.

ISBN: 978-0-262-53419-2

For Neunsie Poody

A burning banknote lights up the scene.
—Konrad Bayer

CONTENTS

SERIES FOREWORD

A short circuit occurs when there is a faulty connection in the network—faulty, of course, from the standpoint of the network's smooth functioning. Is not the shock of short-circuiting, therefore, one of the best metaphors for a critical reading? Is not one of the most effective critical procedures to cross wires that do not usually touch: to take a major classic (text, author, notion), and read it in a short-circuiting way, through the lens of a "minor" author, text, or conceptual apparatus ("minor" should be understood here in Deleuze's sense: not "of lesser quality," but marginalized, disavowed by the hegemonic ideology, or dealing with a "lower," less dignified topic)? If the minor reference is well chosen, such a procedure can lead to insights which completely shatter and undermine our common perceptions. This is what Marx, among others, did with philosophy and religion (short-circuiting philosophical speculation through the lens of political economy, that is to say, economic speculation); this is what Freud and Nietzsche did with morality (short-circuiting the highest ethical notions through the lens of the unconscious libidinal economy). What such a reading achieves is not a simple "desublimation," a reduction of the higher intellectual content to its lower economic or libidinal cause; the aim of such an approach is, rather, the inherent decentering of the interpreted text, which brings to light its "unthought," its disavowed presuppositions and consequences.

And this is what "Short Circuits" wants to do, again and again. The underlying premise of the series is that Lacanian psychoanalysis is a privileged instrument of such an approach, whose purpose is to illuminate a standard text or ideological formation, making it readable in a totally new way—the long history of Lacanian interventions in philosophy, religion, the arts (from the visual arts to the cinema, music, and literature), ideology, and politics justifies this premise. This, then, is not a new series of books on psychoanalysis, but a series of "connections in the Freudian field"—of short

Lacanian interventions in art, philosophy, theology, and ideology. "Short Circuits" intends to revive a practice of reading which confronts a classic text, author, or notion with its own hidden presuppositions, and thus reveals its disavowed truth. The basic criterion for the texts that will be published is that they effectuate such a theoretical short circuit. After reading a book in this series, the reader should not simply have learned something new: the point is, rather, to make him or her aware of another—disturbing—side of something he or she knew all the time.

Slavoj Žižek

ACKNOWLEDGMENTS

This book had its beginning during a two-year residency at JVE Institute in Maastricht as a kind of rapprochement between my philosophical and artistic practice. It was the conditions, encounters, and friendships occasioned by this wonderful and strange institution—a genuine *erewhon* (half squat, half think tank)—that made this book possible. I would like to thank Katja Diefenbach, Mladen Dolar, Dominiek Hoens, Hans-Christian Dany, Nasrin Tabai, Babak Afrassiabi, Imogen Stidworthy, and Koen Brams, each of whose interest in my work greatly impacted this book. Hans-Christian introduced me to the work of Oswald Wiener. Dominiek's invitation to contribute to a volume on Melancholia and Politics resulted in the addition of the figure of the happy melancholic to this motley ensemble. Katja's Luciferian lucidity remains an inspiration. One could argue that the book itself was hatched over coffee with Mladen at the Vrijthof. Without his friendship, intellectual support, and above all, encouragement, this book would still be but a bramble. He is a true model of generosity, of elegance, dignity, and rigor, not only in thinking but in affairs as such.

The book has developed in spits and spatters, and would have been altogether swallowed by the ergasiophobe in me if it were not for the friendship and invitations extended by Nathan Brown. Every writer, I imagine, has a number of choice interlocutors to whom they address their most cherished refinements. Nathan is at the top of my list. The philosophical symposia that he helps to organize annually in collaboration with Petar Milat and Tomislav Medak at MaMa Multimedia Institute in Zagreb have forced more than a few of the thoughts that ended up in this book. I feel honored to count Petar and Tom as friends and interlocutors.

I would also like to thank Helmut Draxler. In its final stages especially, this book was propelled by the excitement and enthusiasm of our conversations.

It is a rare thing indeed to find people, let alone *thinkers*, who traverse disciplinary fields with such ease of movement.

My intellectual and artistic itinerary owes countless debts, but I would like to mention the friends and interlocutors whose voices have helped most to inflect my own during the writing of this book: Elizabeth Abrams, Stefan Abrams, Avi Alpert, R.B., Walter Brogan, Victoria Brooks, David Dempewolf, Marcel Dickhage, Benjamin Fallon, the late Ludwig Fischer, Jeffrey Gower, James Krone, Justin Matherly, Mattin, Cynthia Mitchell, Lesley Moon, Mike Olson, Café Orange in Lovran, Gahee Park, Albrecht Pischel, Charlie Prusik, Gabriel Rockhill, Lisa Rosendahl, Nathania Rubin, Cathleen Schuster, Jan Sieber, Amy Sillman, Charlie Strong, Cheyney Thompson, Mike Vass, Jason Waite, Jeff Weber, Evan Calder Williams, Yuka Yokoyama, Marek Zawisla.

Parts of the book have been published elsewhere. Aspects of chapter 2 first appeared in my "More or Less Art, More or Less a Commodity, More or Less an Object, More or Less a Subject—The Readymade and the Artist," in "The Art of the Concept," ed. Nathan Brown and Petar Milat, *Frakcija Performing Arts Journal*, no. 64/65 (2013), and I recast this chapter in light of a short text entitled "An Object that Speaks" that appeared in *Spike Art Quarterly*, no. 48 (Summer 2016), 50–55. Chapter 7, "The Happy Melancholic," was first published with the same title in "Politics and Melancholia," ed. Justin Clemens and Dominiek Hoens, *Crisis and Critique* 3, no. 2 (2016).

Writing a book is a grueling endeavor. Luckily I have been uniquely charmed to have Amanda Holmes by my side for the vast majority of it. Her love, ferocious intelligence, and sheer ebullience, even during the bloodshot hours of the manuscript's completion, surely kept this book, not to mention myself, from oblivion. Her scrupulous edits challenged this book into its final form, and she proves that dissolute subjects are not without love.

Finally, I am grateful to my family and my father for their love and support. Although I have dedicated this book to my grandmother, Margaret Anderson, it and all my future books should be really dedicated to my mum, Pamela Chapman, whose love and encouragement makes stones buoyant. She is one of the few who truly gives what she does not have.

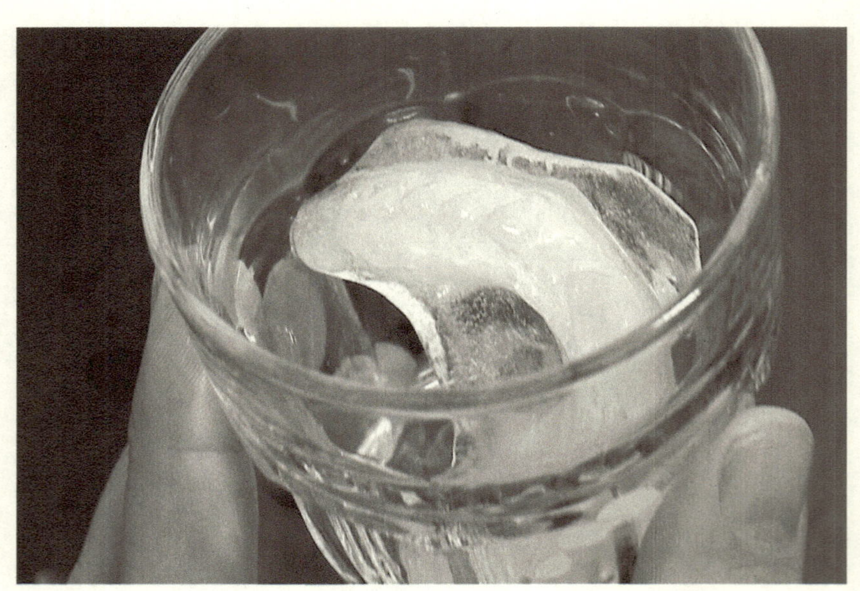

INTRODUCTION

The subjects of this book, like its subject matter, should be taken in earnest.

In Thomas Bernhard's "In Earnest," one of 104 short stories from a collection entitled *The Voice Imitator*, the narrator describes an episode in which a group of Bavarian excursionists encounter at the precipice of a "rocky ledge above the so-called Salzburg horse-pond" a well-known and successful "comic actor who had for decades earned his living by being funny." Suited in "lederhosen and a Tyrolean hat on his head," the actor states his intention of throwing himself off the ledge. Taking the declaration as a joke, the group "as usual burst into laughter." Fulfilling their "long-expected sensation," however, "the actor is reported to have said that he was in earnest and to have immediately thrown himself off."[1]

Like all of the stories in the collection, the narrator adopts a voice at once familiar and strange, a tone banal and horrific, and a humor as dry as the growing desert. Deviations are remarked, catastrophes described with minimal embellishment and without sensation: no shock, no awe. Idiotic and senseless events unfold in variation, subjects run amok, and common phrases such as "in the nature of things" and adjectives like "so-called" are repeated to the point of assuming a vacuous significance. The narrator registers details with *dandyesque* lucidity, as an I coolly detached, Luciferian, even in hatred[2] like an atomist acknowledging the eternal and meaningless rain of atoms within the void. The universe Bernhard constructs is one where things go horribly wrong, accidents happen, crimes are committed, and cruelties perpetrated not as exceptions but as matters of course. Liquidation world: everything must go.

Earnestness—the most priggish of virtues—becomes ridiculous precisely for being uttered without a hint of irony, dryly executed, murdered into insignificance by being quite simply the case. The opposite of Oscar Wilde's prose, whose *The Importance of Being Earnest* abounds in clever plays and ironic twists, the dark humor of Bernhard's stories derives from the manner in which the language is forced into literality, removed from the ease and facility of its sense, of its inattentive deployments, of its capacity to say the opposite. The humor derives from this excessive precision, where the word says itself into oblivion as a drill bit's pitiless repetition bores a hole. Bernhard works toward isolating the non-sense of sense by attending literally to the sense in an effort to reach "the greatest exactitude and the most extreme dissolution."[3] The narrative tone itself assumes a character similar to Gilles Deleuze's treatment of Bartleby the Scrivener's formula *I would prefer not to*: a statement that "means only what it says, literally," becoming an *agrammatical* formula through its repeated utterance that focuses the sense of the statement on its anomalous *ring* as if it were an "inarticulate block, a single breath."[4] Unsurprisingly, each story in Bernhard's book is presented as a single block on a single page. The book of stories is a stack of paragraphs accumulating horizontally in space like Carl Andre's *Lever* (1966).

The story following "In Earnest" in the collection, "Too Much," comprised of a single sentence, is exemplary in this regard for its economy and precision, and its sinisterly sick humor: "A Paterfamilias who had for decades been praised and beloved for a so-called *extraordinary sense of family* and who one Saturday afternoon, admittedly in especially humid weather, murdered four of his six children, defended himself in court by saying that all of a sudden the children were *too much* for him."[5] The children were indeed *too much* for him: an explanation that explains everything by explaining nothing. The understatement of the overstatement pushes the expression in violently opposing directions as if to force the expression to literally understate itself, voiding itself of sense. In such a world where the most horrible has become horribly funny, in such a liquidation world, for things to be taken in earnest requires the earnestness of such quintessentially comic acts. It requires subjects to step off the ledge. Not to say that either suicide or murdering one's children is funny, but that the language that frames these events makes them funny when language itself is removed from its vague capacity for euphemism, when it tries to simply mark the hole in space. The single sentence of a single paragraph of a singular story on a singular page: language, like a thing, is a hole in a thing it is not.

Horror occasions a stripping bare of sense where language's push toward the literal succeeds by failing, when the word becomes a mute obstacle, a stumbling block. Language that makes one trip occasions a thinking that can pronounce on the nothing it marks. The comic actor's comic act is a matter of saying what he does, of being earnest. If its fulfillment renders earnestness ridiculously funny, it is because his act, *throwing himself off*, puts the value of earnestness as such into question.

This is what earnestness should do: it should throw one off. Such earnestness in a comic actor is what is called deadpan. The comic act is a matter of making oneself absent, effecting a separation between an effect caused and the one who caused it. The comic subject is situated in this gap where one (he or she) becomes an object of laughter while refusing to recognize its cause. If Bernhard's comic actor makes comedy by doing what he says, he also makes the sensation expected of him my marking it: it is in earnest, he says. Such comedy is the opposite of lighthearted; it is a heaviness that plummets like the subject that steps off the ledge. Stepping off is a nihilistic act, and not simply because the subject decides that she or he (it) has had it. The nihilism of the act consists in consigning the subject to the weight of the person, that being irreversibly inscribed into that most pivotal law of classical mechanics: the law of gravity. The comic actor, however, does not simply take the plunge but does so *in earnest*, fulfilling language's promise: it meant what *he* said. Language in the comic act says what it does; it removes the subject from its place, leaving that absence into which a whole host of things can be tossed, including one's own person. And the comedy of the act lies in the decision stated in earnest to make the person go along for the ride. It is not the suicide itself that is comic, but its staging, the way in which it draws focus to the hole where the subject goes absentee, and it is this humor—the undeniable truth of its funniness—that marks the hole of sense. The comic actor makes an object of his absence: while his person falls, this object remains.

To make an object of absence: this is the central problem that runs throughout this book and which I often refer to as the absentee or dissolute subject. All of the *subjects* treated in this book internalize a relation to their own absence by making an object of it. This book at its core is a study of a series of such "object-subjects" and the *artistic* practices involved in their elaboration and production. Subjects that relate to themselves as objects, they become impersonators of their own absence. Pervaded by a dark humor, these subjects step off the ledge to mark the place of their absence, that is, the void beneath their feet.

****

Bernhard points to the vertigo of impersonation in the story "The Voice Imitator," which is also the title for the collection of stories as a whole. The narrator recounts an occasion in which a "voice imitator" is invited to Kahlenberg to show off his art, which he does quite brilliantly, faltering only when presented with the request to imitate his own voice: "When, however, at the very end, we suggested that he imitate his own voice, he said he could not do that."[6]

This story should be read at two levels. At the first level, it is an allegory of the impossibility of separating the artist from the singularity of his or her own voice, which, as the medium of imitation cannot itself be imitated by the artist him or herself. The voice of an artist is inimitable precisely because it is produced through a relation to an other voice that is not the author's own. The story itself becomes an allegory of the art of writing as *voice imitation* as such whose singularity—an author's voice—cannot itself be separated from its act of inhabiting a voice. In addition to this allegorical reading, which of course indexes the problem of voice as it functions across the stories in the collection, it also refers to a specific figure, *a* voice imitator, or more familiarly, an impersonator. The story recounts the impossibility of a specific subject, namely that of the voice imitator, imitating its own voice. The "own" here remains ambiguous: it could refer to the person of the voice imitator, i.e., the person the subject is when not engaging in his practice. However, the "own" could also refer to the voice imitator as such, since this character has no other identity within the story. In this case, the voice the "voice imitator" cannot imitate is the act of imitating itself, because it lacks a voice of its own. Translated into the terms of impersonation: the impersonator cannot impersonate the manner in which he or she impersonates. And the problem of authorial voice as it is posed in this collection engages the interminable equivocation in the sense of the voice imitator's "ownness." To stress the impossibility of imitating one's *own* voice—the strange and enigmatic fact that one *can* become a caricature of oneself, but cannot oneself be the one to produce that caricature—cannot be separated from the impossibility of impersonating the act of impersonation. Insofar as we are persons, we are impersonators who neglect to take the "im" of our personations into account. The inimitability of the "own" consists in the "im" and not a presumed personal identity.

So the story and the collection as a whole pose the enigma of the anomalous voice of the one who impersonates. Wherein and in what does the *persona* of the impersonator (the figure who singularly lacks a persona) consist? This incapacity on the part of the voice imitator to imitate his own voice signals the strange truth that voice imitation, and impersonation as such, lie between the third person and the first person. The omnipresent I of Bernhard's novels is constantly marking this displacement in which a one (the third person) is subjectivated: spoken as "I," in the first person. Impersonation consists in the very act of separating the I from its first *personness* by assuming the I (strictly speaking, the me) of an other, which is then spoken in the first person. Since the impersonation is not riveted to any particular other or person, it is the other as such (the Other) that is always implicated in an impersonation: the one who speaks in me. Oddly, an impersonation implies that the I of the impersonator is situated between its person and the impersonal I. This gap enables the impersonator to *personify* the other, and it is this gap that produces something like the inimitability of one's own voice. In this case, the "clever" request for the "voice imitator" to imitate his own voice makes no sense, since he cannot imitate *his* own voice, qua voice imitator, without the other; and since one's "own voice" qua impersonator lies in the "im" of personation, it can only appear through the adoption of an other's inflection: the marking of the singularity and difference between the other and the Other (others that speak and the one who speaks them). There is no voice that would be his own, but it is also nobody else's voice. It is this strange anonymous voice, which is nonetheless singular and inimitable, that the writer (and let's here assert, the artist as such) seeks. The artist-writer as an impersonator, as a voice imitator, is a subject that has no person. The impersonator is situated in the gap between the person (the persona of the other) and their own im(*non*)personality.

A decisive consequence must be drawn. Impersonation does not confirm but abolishes reflexivity: the circuit that at least syntactically allows one to say both I and me. In positioning oneself as the other, one establishes not one's own identity but paradoxically one's nonidentity in the adoption of a persona. An impersonation (personification of the other) implies an impersonation (of the self). One becomes a person only by separating oneself from one's own subjectivity, situating the gap between it and the person. What one accepts as reflexivity is in fact an impersonation of the gap between that which differentiates the persona and the subject.

****

A "comedian" like Andy Kaufman *consists* as a subject through the manner in which he plays with the relation between personhood (personal identity) and the impersonal. His *act* lies in identifying his *own* person with an impersonation. His performances—as strange as they are funny—present the subject as absent: a placeholder of a vacancy attached to an unconvincing person. We neither believe nor disbelieve in the identity of the figures he presents (Foreign Man or Tony Clifton or the many variations of himself, Andy). They are beyond belief, not in the sense of being unbelievable but in that, as is perhaps most clear in Kaufman's "self"-appearance, the persons do not appear to be present, even when appearing *in person*, so to speak. It is as if the *person* he is has become completely identified with the "im" of personation. As if, impersonating his own absence, the singularity of his person attaches itself to the absence it marks.

Despite his claims to the contrary, Andy Kaufman is indeed a comedian. Yet the necessity of adding this "indeed" belies an uncertainty that infects the judgment, tipping it toward the interrogative: is he indeed a comedian? The strangeness of Kaufman's humor—his not-funny funniness—lies in his uncanny ability to wrong-step the audience, thwarting any attempt to categorize his performance. As Julie Hecht reports: "'I just want the audience to have a wonderful, happy feeling inside them and leave with big smiles on their faces,' Andy told me with a blank stare the first time I met him. 'I can't help if people laugh, I'm not trying to be funny,' he explained. He said that he felt insulted when he saw reviews calling him a comedian."[7] Yet his desire not to be taken seriously as a comedian—"I'm just a simple entertainer ... I just want to put smiles on people's faces"—is undermined by his comic ambition—"I wouldn't mind being compared to Charlie Chaplin or W. C. Fields." To take comedy seriously, that is to say, *in earnest*, one has to not be a comedian. And his relation to Marcel Duchamp, in this regard, has not gone unremarked.[8] Put differently, to take comedy seriously, one cannot be serious about being a comedian. This is Andy Kaufman's strange ambition, *to take comedy seriously, that is, in earnest*. He, too, steps off the ledge, or, as he prefers, *goes too far*.[9]

If comedy is fundamentally a wound to seriousness, then how can the comedian take what he or she is doing seriously? The false solution to this dilemma would be to simply ham it up, to play the fool, to not commit oneself to what one does: I am a comedian; therefore I am not to be taken seriously. Kaufman's solution is curious: I am not a comedian; therefore I am to be taken seriously (as a comedian). Kaufman assumes an identity that can only be affirmed through its disavowal. And it is this paradox that he unfolds with unsurpassable rigor. What he articulates, if one follows the logic of his performance, is that comedy consists in *miscognition*. The act of comedy undermines being *a* comedian, since comedy itself consists in the frustration of the logic of identification. To make comedy requires standing in the place of one's own absence. To be painfully consistent, the comedian has to be a noncomedian, since comedy consists in the separation of the subject from its role, from its persona. The purest form of comedy, Kaufman proposes, is in fact impersonation. The impersonator is not *one* with its appearance. Yet, rather than comfortably assuming the role of the entertainer as one who is not *one* with how they appear—which assumes that there is an identity behind the appearance, a real me behind the role—Kaufman states: I am not one with how I appear because one is not one. Conversely, he says, this is me, I am me, there is no other I than this me here.

His *act* turns on an incessant play with and on negation, in which he thwarts any attempt to either identify him with his role or distance him from it. If he is not a comedian, it is because he is a comic *impersonator*: an impersonator of the comedian. Kaufman's genius lies in the manifold ways in which he plays with the logic of impersonation. Neither the ventriloquist nor the impersonator is an actor in the classical sense.[10] Whereas an actor is defined by the assumption of a character whose success consists in maintaining the difference between the actor and his or her mask (*persona*), the impersonator, as the word itself suggests, is less a matter of assuming or forging a character than of distancing oneself from one's own character. The assumption of a persona implies the deformation, if not destruction, of one's own. To impersonate suggests a separation from one's own person, and it is this separation that Kaufman exhibits in exemplary manner. One of his first "characters," significantly enough, is an impersonator himself whose identity is that of a nondescript "foreign man." Foreign Man's act consists chiefly of jokes without punch lines and impersonations almost all of which are abominable until he proposes to do "*the* Elvis Presley," whom he then impersonates with an uncanny genius. Foreign Man is a figure that makes people laugh when he does not intend to and produces awkward silence when he intends to make people laugh. He is a subject who does not know the rules of the game and is constantly failing (e.g., his appearance as "Baji Kimran" in 1978 on *The Dating Game*, where his "failing" is precisely being *earnest*). He is always an object of laughter and never a subject. Kaufman, to force language a bit, *impersonifies the person*. Erecting a comic identity on the ruins of the person, Kaufman relentlessly exposes the "im" of personation.

****

The comic actor, the impersonator, and Andy Kaufman—these exemplary instances of dissolute subjectivity—all take their absence earnestly. They no longer believe in the integrity of the person. In this sense, they provide a means of introduction to the concerns of this book. They are exemplars that portend a series of exemplary instances to come and whose theoretical portraits I wish to sketch. If I stress the notion of portraiture, it is because in each chapter a kind of subject is at stake—an absentee subject—that finds its locus or loci in the objects that absent it. Each chapter is a sketch of a subject and an attempt to think the manner in which it absents itself.

The book traverses a series of artistic and literary figures and a range of types. It begins with a sustained consideration of Marcel Duchamp's apparatus of the *Stoppages* as a means to orient thought within the medium of its own disorientation (chapter 1), then proceeds to touch on the strange comedy of Marcel Broodthaers's sustained meditation on the conundrum of being an art object (chapter 2). The theme of the comic introduced with Broodthaers then opens onto two chapters that develop the notion of the comic subject: the *umouristic* subject treats the inimitable Jacques Vaché (chapter 3), while the ridiculous subject takes its departure from Alfred Jarry's pistol (chapter 4). The nihilist as a figure that counts for nothing passes by way of Valéry's *Monsieur Teste* (chapter 5) to an interpretation of the dandy inspired by Oswald Wiener's singular engagement with this figure (chapter 6). The final chapter approaches Baudelaire as the happy melancholic (chapter 7).

Although the practices differ, I have chosen them because each assumes from the outset a subject that is *sick*, to use Freud's terminology. These subjects are sick in the specific sense that they assume the absence of meaning and the liquidation of value. In a letter to his good friend Marie Bonaparte, on August 13, 1937, Freud writes:

> The moment a man questions the meaning and value of life, he is sick, since objectively neither has any existence; by asking this question one is merely admitting to a store of unsatisfied libido to which something else must have happened, a kind of fermentation leading to sadness and depression. I am afraid these explanations of mine are not very wonderful. Perhaps because I am too pessimistic. I have an advertisement floating about in my head which I consider the boldest and most successful piece of American publicity: "Why live, if you can be buried for ten dollars?"[11]

The subjects taken up in the following chapters all accept as an axiom of thought the *not very wonderful*. They are all haunted, like Freud, by this audacious query fit for advertising the bleak terrain of the spaghetti Western: *Why live, if you can be buried for ten dollars?*

This book should be of concern, I hope, to all of us who take this ill-defined activity, the practice we call thought, seriously, that is *in earnest*. Knowing full well its fragility and the ease with which it is snuffed out, these figures each consign subjectivity to thought as a means of sustaining or propping up their own absence in a world where "life is not a sacred thing, to be protected by force of arms if necessary, but an intrinsically worthless commodity."[12] They concern themselves with art, with thought, without assuming its value or meaning from the outset. They begin from a point of utter debasement, from what Marx terms, in a moment of impolite lucidity, the "universal prostitution ... of personal talents, capacities, abilities, activities."[13] Only a subject fundamentally disoriented, thrown off axis, unanchored, only a subject that assumes the world as liquidated of all meaning, of all value, would indeed assume the peculiar task of making an object of their absence.

Emblems of absence, these subjects sustain thought in deeply grim times. This book, if nothing else, is a document of a commitment, to borrow a wonderful phrase from Harold Pinter, to accept *nothing from the bargain basement*. Thinking is a matter of "leaving no stone unturned and no maggot lonely."[14] A thinking that takes the void as its medium is buoyant. Democritus after all is the laughing philosopher. Far from being crushed by the void's depressive weight, the subject that makes an object of its absence grasps the earnestness of the comic.

CHAPTER 1

THE METROLOGIST: ON MARCEL DUCHAMP'S *THREE STANDARD STOPPAGES*

To make an artwork that is not a work of art ... This is the problem that Duchamp poses for himself and whose now infamous solution is the readymade—a term that he came up with in 1915 shortly after his arrival in New York. The readymade is the result, as Duchamp puts it, of a *rendez-vous*—a chance encounter—in which a prefabricated object, a commodity, is nominated, and it is this name, or better, the act of naming, that institutes it as *art*. The act of nominating a readymade marks the object, cuts into it, separating it from what it is: a particular object, composed of an array of qualities, of use values as Marx would have it, to which its substance is indelibly attached. This act reinscribes the object, setting it apart by placing it in relation to "art" (art discourse, i.e., the judgments that allow something to be discerned and thus recognized as art) so as to reduce art to non-art. As if placed into a hole—occupying the place of its own absence—the readymade marks the hole as it plugs it, to allude to one of Duchamp's last readymades, *Drainstopper* (*Bouche-évier*). The act of naming is a decision that decides on its being art, cutting the object *pataphysically* by relating the object through this act to that which it is not (this thing we call art). Not *this*: a commodity encountered in the marketplace; not *that*: an art object. Its nomination is a decision, but it is a decision that is essentially (not accidentally) indecisive. It is a decision to *make* art by not making art.

It is this essential negativity that interests Duchamp. In an interview with Pierre Cabanne, he describes this negativity as an encounter that produces an aesthetic indifference:

> **CABANNE:** How did you come to choose a mass-produced object, a "readymade," to make a work of art?
>
> **DUCHAMP:** Please note that I did not want to make a work of art out of it. The word "readymade" did not appear until 1915, when I went to the United States. It was an interesting word, but when I put a bicycle wheel on a stool, the fork

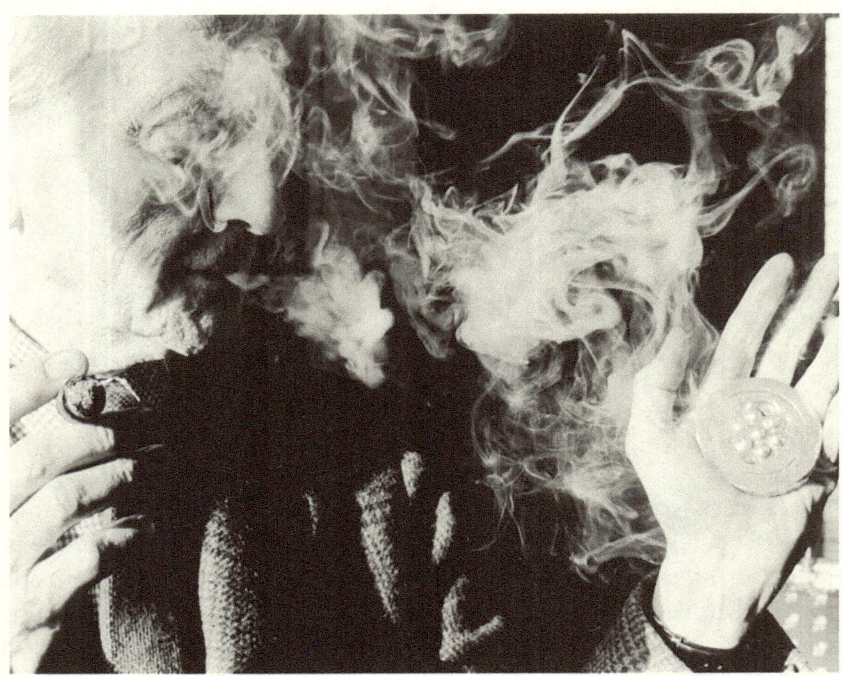

FIGURE 1.1
International Collectors Society, sale brochure cover, 1967. Marcel Duchamp showing *The Marcel Duchamp Art Medal* based on *Drain Stopper*. Courtesy of the Philadelphia Museum of Art

> down, there was no idea of a "readymade," or anything else. It was just a distraction. I didn't have any special reason to do it, or any intention of showing it, or describing anything. ... The word "readymade" thrust itself on me then. It seemed perfect for these things that weren't works of art, that weren't sketches, and to which no art terms applied. That's why I was tempted to make them.
>
> **CABANNE:** What determined your choice of readymades?
>
> **DUCHAMP:** That depended on the object. In general I had to be aware of its "look." It's very difficult to choose an object, because at the end of fifteen days, you begin to like it or hate it. You have to approach something with an indifference, as if you had no aesthetic emotion. The choice of readymades is always based on visual indifference and, at the same time, on the total absence of good and bad taste.[1]

Even if the object is destined to become a work of art (and this is indubitable and in every way decisive), Duchamp insists that the encounter is one of indifference. By this, the play of the faculties, as Kant would put it, that serves to orient all thought is reduced to a zero degree, a null point; to borrow a formula from Deleuze's reading of Melville's "Bartleby," "a negativism beyond all negation."[2] This indifference is the result of an encounter in which the object is not what it is, and in so being, it is what it is not: as such, it is not not-art. It becomes art only at the cost of reducing art to the emptiness of a name that signifies a mere relation to that which it is not. And yet it is this relation that founds a radically new practice of art as a generic practice. As such, it is the event that conditions what we call contemporary art.

The operation of the readymade which situates art within the nullity of its own occurrence—the vertigo of its own immanence—and that is indexed to the problem of making an artwork that is not an artwork—obviously strictly impossible, but whose impossibility is charged with producing a new practice of art—depends upon an encounter in which one is not an artist, that is, not the fabricator of the object, but becomes an artist as an effect of the encounter with the object. It is an encounter that separates the "artist" from his or her taste (*goût*)—the perceptual and cognitive habits that enable one to "recognize" art; to become an artistic subject—to practice art in the generic sense—one's eye and mind have to be separated. A separation that has its locus in Duchamp's insistence on his disgust with the "hand." As Thierry de Duve writes, "Disgusted, and angry, and 'vengeful' toward the hand: we cannot keep track of all the instances when Duchamp declared, as he did to Otto Hahn, that he wanted to 'demonetize the idea of the hand.'"[3] "My hand became my enemy in 1912," Duchamp writes to Francis Roberts, "I wanted to get away from the palette."[4] And the first of Duchamp's pure readymades, *Bottlerack* (*Égouttoir*), is a play on the French *goût* (taste). It is not technique as such that Duchamp finds so repugnant but "touch": the touch of the artist. The very notion of the readymade, as Linda Henderson suggests, may have its basis in the transvaluation of the notion of the already made (*tout fait*) that one finds in the writing of Bergson, where the latter opposes the cold, external, objective gaze of scientific intellect that judges according to "ready-made" ideas to the sensitivity of the artistic act that expresses the "fundamental self."[5] When transposed from science to art, rejecting "ready-made" ideas rejects the notions of the sensitive artist and the expressive self.[6]

Duchamp's readymade is comical insofar as it makes literal his acceptance of the objective, cold, external gaze characteristic of the scientific intellect. By taking an object already made, industrially produced, and not the result of the artist's craft or an artistic sensibility, Duchamp not only accepts as a starting point the radical externality of the self to itself (its alienation), but makes the very problem of art's objectivity into a problem of and for the subject of art and of the subject guided by "ready-made" notions, such as the idea of a métier. Paradoxically the readymade requires that one jettison subjectivity in order then to jettison objectivity in art. Addressing a ready-made object rather than a ready-made idea, the artist does not make the art object but the art idea, which assigns a measureless measure to art. The paradoxical solution of the readymade is that it makes the immeasurable into the very measure of art. What is to be made is not the object but the subject of art, that is, the subject that apprehends and thereby decides upon it. Yet this subject cannot be given "ready-made," so to speak. It does not precede but proceeds from the decision it makes. If the readymade marks Duchamp's definitive break with the "hand" (the subjective in art)—separating the artist from what he or she can do (the artist is not a painter, a sculptor, etc., but an artist, a generic vocation)—and likewise separates art from an essence (the objective in art)—lacking a definition, art becomes an operation that produces a subject that recognizes something as art—it poses the problem of art as one of measurement or lack thereof. The problem of measurement lies at the heart of Duchamp's "artistic" concern and assumes a sense not dissimilar to the one that Protagoras gives it: "the human being is the measure [*metron*] of all things [*panton chremeton*]." By this I do not intend merely the banality that Duchamp makes the artist into the measure of all things artistic. Rather, the artist shoulders the difficult task of internalizing a measureless measure. Measure in this sense concerns the proper limit, the criterion through which something can be said to be or not be.[7] Through the problem of measure, Duchamp problematizes the very idea of art. What he does is show not only that there is not an intrinsic measure to art, that nothing is proper to art (and he pursues this in the direction that leads him to question the very notion of intrinsic measures as such), but that art *exhausts* measurement.

To exhaust measurement is not a matter of transgressing the limit of the measurable, of asserting the importance or value of that which exceeds all measurement. To exhaust measure is rather to violate the rule of good or proper measurement that states that there are things that can be measured and others that cannot be. To exhaust measurement exhausts its *possibility* by exhausting that which is measurable in measurement itself. It measures, paradoxically, by means of the immeasurable.[8] Art becomes a matter of making a measure and not simply taking a measurement, but what it makes into a measure is the not-measurable. Paradoxically, art becomes its own measure only insofar as it singularly lacks measurability. If the readymade is a consequence of this exhaustion, its precursor, *Three Standard Stoppages* (1913–1914), is a work that presents itself literally as a measure and in which Duchamp comically presents the artist as a metrologist, making use of the form of science to demystify art and art to demystify science.

****

Marcel Duchamp's *Three Standard Stoppages* treats art as an apparatus of measurement and measurement as an apparatus of art. Neither a painting nor a drawing nor sculpture, the medium of the *Stoppages*, as Duchamp claimed, is chance itself; chance being both the thing to be measured and the new standard of measurement. In a note from the 1914 Box, Duchamp describes "The Idea of the Fabrication" as follows: "If a straight horizontal thread one meter long falls from a height of one meter straight onto a horizontal plane, distorting itself *as it pleases*, and creates a new shape of the measure of length."[9] Duchamp would shortly thereafter execute this procedure, or at least claim to have executed it, by holding a meter-long piece of thread at the height of one meter, letting it drop onto pieces of canvas that he had painted Prussian blue. Repeating the procedure three times—to give the necessary semblance of order—Duchamp then fixed each of the distortions onto the canvas with drops of varnish. The next phase of the work was completed while working on *Tu m'* (1918), his last painting on canvas. Using each stoppage as a model, he had wooden templates cut which could then be used as rulers. And Duchamp purportedly made use of these "rulers" in a number of works. He completed the *Stoppages* in 1936 while preparing it for exhibition at the Museum of Modern Art: cutting each stoppage into a thin strip and mounting them on glass panes and then housing all of the elements in the croquet box—a decision that drives home comically the allusion to the platinum standard meter kept in the International Bureau for Measure and Weights in Sèvres, France.

If the work's medium is chance, the contingency of the swerve (to allude to the ancient wisdom of Lucretius) that gives rise to form, to shape, the function or role of the artist is simply to register it objectively, to be the servant or instrument of its pleasure, its mechanical will; the fall of the string *produces form as it pleases*. And the artist is reduced to drawing the consequences. This play on the sense of "drawing" certainly did not escape Duchamp. Aping the form of the metrologist, the task of the artist is to ground art in chance. The work then is nothing but the objectification of chance.

The *Stoppages* is Duchamp's most profound foray into the pataphysical. Alfred Jarry defines pataphysics in four key ways: "the science of imaginary solutions"; "a science of the particular"; a science examining "the laws governing exceptions"; and "a science of that which is superinduced upon metaphysics, whether within or beyond the latter's limitations, extending as far beyond metaphysics as the latter extends beyond physics," that "stands to metaphysics as metaphysics stands to physics."[10] As a pataphysical device, the *Stoppages* is an imaginary solution to a physical impossibility: the measurement of chance. One can produce the calculus of a chance occurrence's probability, but the throw of the dice does not abolish chance as such. The event itself, the swerve, is contingent; it is an utterly singular occurrence bound up with its materiality. One can take its measure only by relating it. This relation suffices to abolish it, registering it as a nullity. To take the measure of chance demands the abolishment of the measure. To imagine the measure of chance is to take the measure of the immeasurable.

To ground art in the pataphysical science of imaginary measurement results in a contradictory object: a measure that produces a measure incommensurable with the concept of measurement (the measurement of the immeasurable). Pataphysics is not a science of contradiction but a contradictory science. Grounding art through such a science likewise induces a paradox. An art that is pataphysical will deploy a technique (intention) that is nontechnical (nonintentional). The *Stoppages* presents itself as a technical apparatus that has the effect of eliminating artistic technique (artistic intention). The pataphysical apparatus of the *Stoppages* produces a new theoretical object (inconsistent with science) and a new theoretical subject (inconsistent with art). The pataphysical grounds art in its singular occurrence (a science of true particularity): in the very gap between physical determination (that which can be conceptually determined, schematized in the Kantian sense) and the metaphysical (understood as the determination of beings as such and as a whole). If Deleuze can maintain, as he does, that Martin Heidegger is a pataphysical thinker and that Jarry is an unrecognized precursor to Heidegger, it is because pataphysics determines the ground of beings through the thought of being, understood as that which conceals itself in its very appearance as *a* being. Being appears as a being (as this or that), but it shows itself in its singularity. The pataphysical, as Deleuze suggests, is a phenomenology of the singular and institutes itself through drawing a distinction between the appearance and the phenomenon: "The phenomenon, on this account, does not refer to a consciousness, but to a Being, the Being of the phenomenon that consists precisely in its self-showing [*se montrer*]. The Being of the phenomenon is the 'epiphenomenon,' non-useful and unconscious, the object of pataphysics."[11] Pataphysics thinks being as chance (singular occurrence, aleatory encounter), which withdraws from all objectification and is hidden in the form it induces.

Through pataphysics, Duchamp aestheticizes science in order to de-aestheticize art. He thereby traces a "new" art object that can be thought but not known (to appeal to the distinction first drawn by Kant between thought and the understanding and radicalized by Heidegger when he distinguishes thought and philosophy). This is what Duchamp calls the nonretinal: an object of an intelligent art (Duchamp's preferred nomenclature), an art that is not "dumb" like painting.

****

There is something genuinely humorous about this strategy of "aestheticizing" science in order to liberate art from the aesthetic. Duchamp himself describes the *Stoppages* as a "joke about the meter." The work takes its departure, quite literally, from the meter as the standard unit of measure. In using the meter as a ground for a new measurement, he regrounds the meter and measurement as such in that which it excludes from all measurement: namely the *act* of measurement itself. Here we see Duchamp's pataphysical brilliance in all its luster. If the piece has to be understood as a joke whose punch line discredits "science mildly, lightly, unimportantly," as Duchamp puts it, this discrediting is pataphysical. Its seriousness does not consists in its scientific skepticism, but in the manner in which Duchamp takes the measure at its word. The *Stoppages* is not funny, but "violently comical" in the sense in which Deleuze formulates it: "it means only what it says, literally."[12]

What does Duchamp do? He uses the measure (the standard meter) to make a measurement, but he does not use it in its intended sense. He does not measure something. Rather he measures nothing. He uses the measure improperly. He does not make use of its form: the end for which it was fashioned. Rather he uses its matter (its literal quantity, its material length). Rather than using the meter to make a measurement, he makes a new measure, a new standard of measurement. Duchamp does not abide by the rules of good measure, which imply, of course, that the meter be used for the sake of making the measure. Duchamp takes this rule quite literally, reading it to the letter. He uses the measure for the sake of *making* the measure. He thus takes the measure of the measure, forcing it to literally do what it says it does. This is the literalization of its rule. It has the effect of reducing the measure to non-sense, and one can only take the measure of the "new" measure through the production of new measures, which is no doubt, in my view, the central import of the fact that there are three stoppages. Just as Frege shows that one cannot say the sense of what one is saying without formulating a new proposition to say it, thus proliferating sense, one cannot take the measure of the measure without creating a new measure. Thus, Duchamp creates a "sign" of measurement: a pataphysical sign. Yet such a sign does not designate or signify; or it signifies only itself (self-referentially) by *showing* itself. It *is* the measure, not a sign of it. It is a measure that can only be shown, presented but not represented. It can never be treated as a means for measuring; it is its own ground, an end in itself.

If we treat the meter as a "standard," the pataphysics of measurement critiques the metaphysics of measurement. The measure necessarily forgets or conceals its relation to the immeasurable—its relation to that which it is not—and this "not" does not admit of measure. Each measure includes within itself an uncertainty that indexes its imperfection, its deviation from the ideal it incarnates. This sleight of hand is not merely accidental but necessary, if it is going to serve its function as the *standard* of measurement. Duchamp exposes the reifying nature of standardization by stripping the meter of its use value, of its essential *quality*; if we are used to treating its essential quality *as a quantity that can be used*, Duchamp perverts this procedure by treating its quantity as a quality. This quality of the *act* of measuring is necessarily concealed by the creation of its intended function or use that presupposes a determination of the limit of the measure, the cut that installs the measure as the representative of the measure.

This limit, this cut, is the notion of stoppage. The problem of measure in art (as with metrology) is bound up with the *art* of measurement, which is a matter of stoppage. By impersonating the metrologist, Duchamp approaches art anachronistically as a question of *techne* (know-how). He treats both the artist and the metrologist as artisans, with sets of skills (techniques), and it is precisely the question of skill that Plato thinks implies the problem of measure. The one who practices the art of measuring would be the technician of technicians, the philosopher. For Plato the problem of measure is posed by those who practice an art (*techne*), for it is only insofar as they are in possession of a *proper* measure that they can practice their art, as a horse trainer must know what is good for a horse in order to train it. If this measure did not exist (if there were not a measurable difference between what is good and bad for horses), then horses could not be trained. Without knowing the "due measure," one cannot grasp what is "fitting" for horses. As the "visitor" says to the young Socrates in the *Statesman*: "There is in fact an art of measurement relating to everything that comes into being. … For it is indeed the case, in a certain way, that all the products of the various sorts of expertise share in measurement."[13] Yet the *Stoppages* inverts the Platonic inquiry. For Plato the problem of measurement serves to ground the knowledge that the technician possesses; for Duchamp, on the contrary, posing the problem of measurement will serve to separate the problem of art from that of *techne*; it will serve to unground, to destabilize what the artist presumes to know. It is chance that undoes this hinge. For whereas Plato inhabits a cosmos where chance as such does not exist, everything having its proper place, its proper measure, grounded ultimately in that which is beyond all measure (the Good beyond being), for Duchamp chance undoes propriety. With the *Stoppages*, he grounds the measurement of art in chance; an operation that will unground measurement, for chance itself will not only be immeasurable but imperfect.

Duchamp claims that the notion of stoppage occurred to him while on a stroll on the rue Claude Bernard in Paris when he encountered the sign *stoppage* above a tailor's shop. That Duchamp himself chose thread (the stitch) for his "experiment" is hardly beside the point. In French, *stoppage* has both the sense that it has in English of "coming to a halt" and the additional meaning of being an "invisible mend" (the utopia of tailors). The process of standardization has the effect of being an invisible stitch, for the measure itself conceals the fact that it required an act of measurement. As with the structure of natural, which is to say metaphysical, illusions in Kant, the mind has the tendency to treat the measure as if it were a thing and not a relation. One treats the meter as if it were a thing, objectively present, simply given, which can in turn be used for the sake of measuring. One does not grasp in the thing its institution. Its apparent stasis (the line marked on the meter bar delimiting what a meter is) is in fact the result of a movement, an act of constitution that, of course, did not have the "meter" to which it could refer. The meter itself should be understood as a dynamic tension, as if it were a string held taut. If the meter sets the measure of truth, establishing a relation that can thereafter be thought as a base unit, then the meter itself, as Henri Poincaré suggests, and whom Duchamp himself had read with great interest, is neither true nor false. It can be neither proven nor falsified, since it becomes the ground for the determination of the true and the false. There is thus an irreducible contingency to the genesis of the measure, bound up with its *act*, the act of taking the measure, which, after it has been set or established, i.e., standardized, appears as something necessary, an unshakeable foundation. The play of sense within the French word *stoppage* no doubt suggested to Duchamp that the meter itself (the standard of standards) seems to have been something tailored: the essential and irreducible gap between its necessity and its contingency mended invisibly. It is thus a piece of art (an artifact). Its whole display serves to reinforce its appearance of perfection: its ideality reinforced, bolstered by its staging. And yet this visible display, which serves its authority, also serves to conceal the imperfections, no matter how slight, that mar its ideality irreparably.

****

Duchamp knows full well that, for the measure to work (to fulfill its function), this seam has to remain invisible; it has to be stopped up, if I can force a bit of French into the English connotation. The art of measurement lies in concealing itself as an art (*techne*), for without this sleight of hand the standard itself would not be set. In this sense, it is metaphysical; it is an art that cannot appear as such, lest its credibility be shaken. The metaphysics of measurement commits it to an infinite horizon of perfectibility.[14] The more refined the technique, the better, the more seamless, the illusion. The scientist is then the most refined of artisans, and is nothing without his or her technique. However, if one is not to be distracted from the seam, one cannot commit oneself to the art of measurement nor remain faithful to the consistency of logic. As Heine suggested, in a poem about Hegel that Freud often liked to quote:

> Life and the world's too fragmented for me!
> A German professor can give me the key.
> He puts life in order with skill magisterial,
> Builds a rational system for better or worse;

> With nightcap and dressing-gown scraps for material
> He chinks up the holes in the universe.[15]

The artist, in this sense, has nothing on the scientist as the inventor of beautiful illusions. The *Stoppages* seems to be animated by this resolutely Nietzschean insight. If the scientist is more artful, a better technician, than the artist can ever hope to be, then the artist can either become a scientist—reaffirming the relation that was forged during the Renaissance with the emergence and refinement of perspective—or make art pit itself against technical refinement, making an "enemy" of the hand. Or is there, perhaps, a third option? In *The New Introductory Lectures*, Freud alludes to Heine's poem:

> [Philosophy] departs from [science] by clinging to the illusion of being able to present a picture of the universe which is without gaps and is coherent. ... It goes astray in its method by over-estimating the epistemological value of our logical operations. ... And it often seems that the poet's derisive comment is not unjustified when he says of the philosopher: "*Mit seinen Nachtmützen und Schlafrockfetzen / Stopft er die Lücken des Weltenbaus*. [With his nightcaps and the tatters of his dressing gown he patches up the gaps in the structure of the universe.]"[16]

Freud presents an image of science stripped of its metaphysical artifice, a science that refuses to present a coherent picture of the universe, refusing to overestimate the value of our logical constructions. Duchamp like Freud will marshal this poetic incisiveness against the philosopher's will to coherence, laboring to make visible the invisible stitches that sustain the belief in the world as an integral whole.

The *Stoppages* plays with reopening and closing this gap, this seam that logical reality must close in order that its machinations do not come to a halt. Thus, stoppage itself should be understood as that which halts movement, interrupts the fall of the string, giving it a permanent shape or form (an ideal appearance fixed for all time), transforming contingency into necessity; standardization as stoppage, as the cessation of movement, the end of an act. And yet it exposes itself (a bride stripped bare) as an interruption: as a measure, it is necessarily contingent. Its contingency lies not in the ideality of the genesis of form but in the manner in which all form is indexed to the non-sense of "taking place." The sense of *this* art "posits" as its necessary condition the nonanteriority of meaning. The *Stoppages* in the end is a pataphysical experiment that grounds a Lucretian physics:

> Thus it will have been noticed that this philosophy is, in sum, a philosophy of the *void*: not only the philosophy which says that the void pre-exists the atoms that fall in it, but a philosophy which creates the philosophical void

> [*fait le vide philosophique*] in order to endow itself with existence: a philosophy which, rather than setting out from the famous "philosophical problems" (why is there something rather than nothing?), begins by evacuating all philosophical problems, hence by refusing to assign itself any "object" whatever ("philosophy has no object") in order to set out from *nothing*, and from the infinitesimal aleatory variation of nothing constituted by the swerve of the fall. Is there a more radical critique of all philosophy, with its pretension to utter the truth about things?[17]

In founding art on chance, Duchamp founds it on the void. Art founds itself not through an appeal to any kind of authority outside itself (to science), but on its own lack of authority. For Duchamp the modern artist has to come to grips with this lack; the artist can rely on nothing but the emptiness of art's name as indexed to the ultimate vacuity of its capacities.

This is the cost of art's commitment to the immanence of its measure, a judgment wagered on its own indifference. If the Cartesian *cogito* effectively seals its foundation within itself, becoming the presuppositionless beginning necessary for science to ground its universal pretensions, the Duchampian *cogito* is split by chance that serves to separate the artist from his or her own capacities, his or her essential possibility qua artist/artisan, in order to think an impossible object. The line that divides the Duchampian *cogito* is curved. It is attached to the event of its being drawn; neither here nor there, neither inside nor outside, providing no orientation outside its own event, its act of taking place. The Duchampian *cogito* is a true travesty of the meter, its non-symmetrical shadow, making use of its authority to found a "system" whose extension is singular: as if trying to speak with a language of proper names. The only system of measurement which in fact could fulfill its own requirements would not be a system at all, since its universality would coincide with its singularity (a name that would only name itself; a measure that could only measure itself). Duchamp exposes the measure's symbolic import, namely that it founds itself through those subjected to it. In becoming subject to its law, one thus recognizes it and is gripped by its constraining objectivity. Yet, like the space of perspective in painting, its illusion only appears to those who occupy the place of its projection. It is a view from a perspective whose objectivity is founded on the emptiness of the subject who occupies the point external to the picture plane. The meter, just like the scientific pretensions of perspective, depends on establishing the symmetry between the inside and the outside of that which the measure measures.

If perspective subordinates the line to the subject which must hold it taut at the end of the visual pyramid, Duchamp's subject lets the line slacken, releasing it from its constraint, opening it to contingency. One can imagine the picture plane whose axes (x, y, z) are diverted by their fall, warping the Euclidean space of one-point perspective. This effect of warping is already registered in Cézanne's distortion of perspective (the strange effect of bulging that is often noted). Yet if Cézanne's importance lies in a form of painting that breaches the requisite distance of the perspectival subject from the eye, placing it in things (the eye's palpation, as Merleau-Ponty describes so well), Duchamp's operation displaces the space of the picture altogether. It is not merely the decentered, impersonal subject of the visible that interests him but a subject that situates itself at that point of radical indifference which threatens the collapse of all distinction, all measure: art can be everything or nothing. Only a subject that will invest in its own nothingness will back art. Duchamp's line is abstract in the sense that Deleuze articulates it at the beginning of *Difference and Repetition*: "The abstract line acquires all its force from giving up the model—that is to say, the plastic symbol of the form—and participates in the ground all the more violently in that it distinguishes itself from it without the ground distinguishing itself from the line."[18] The chance operation generates a nonlinear line whose form is not governed by an intention. Duchamp's procedure liberates the line from its strict measure (loosening it); if the meter is indeed the paradigmatic image of a line ordered by a rule, the *Stoppages* serves to standardize a disoriented line, a line thrown off its axis. The procedure liberates the meter from its own standard, subordinating the "magnitude" of its measure to the incalculable. Inaugurating a form of thought at home in its disorientation, Duchamp's greatness is that he drew from it very personal consequences, bequeathing to each artist the task of tracing a *cogito* of his or her own.

CHAPTER 2

THE OBJECT-SUBJECT: MARCEL BROODTHAERS, MERCHANT OF THE INSINCERE

> In earlier times, I wrote poems, concrete signs of engagement, since there was no compensation. Therefore, my work consisted of writing as little as possible. Now, with the plastic arts, I can only engage with my adversaries, and I try to produce as much of nothingness and indifference as possible. This space can only lead us to paradise.[1]

In 1962 the poet Marcel Broodthaers met the artist Piero Manzoni on the occasion of the latter's exhibition at Galerie Aujourd'hui in Brussels. A meeting of two comedians, as Broodthaers would later describe it. Manzoni presented Broodthaers with a certificate (no. 71) authenticating him as work of art: "This is to certify that Marcel Broodthaers has been signed by my hand and therefore has to be considered as an authentic work of art for all intents and purposes as of the date below. Brussels, 23-2-62 Piero Manzoni."[2] The following year Broodthaers would decide to become artist, actively distancing himself from his identity as poet. Manzoni would die of a heart attack.

In a text written shortly after Manzoni's death, Broodthaers jokingly attributes the latter's physical demise "to the attitude he had adopted on the artistic level."[3] If this attitude, tending toward the comically morose, lands Manzoni in "the terrible book of the 20th century," producing an art so dark, a comedy so uneasy, that it provokes a revenge of the real, it is because this attitude assumes the full consequences of a radically dystopian position of the artist: in a culture so corrupted that even the production of shit (real or fictional), that most abject of readymades, could pass as art. Indexing his tins of artist's shit to the price of gold, Manzoni highlights art's tawdry alchemy, its capacity to produce something from nothing, making the artist a magician and a confidence man, or, as Broodthaers prefers, a merchant of the insincere.

Like Manzoni, Broodthaers takes his departure from the "superimposition," as he later puts it, "of artistic and commercial values."[4] Broodthaers and

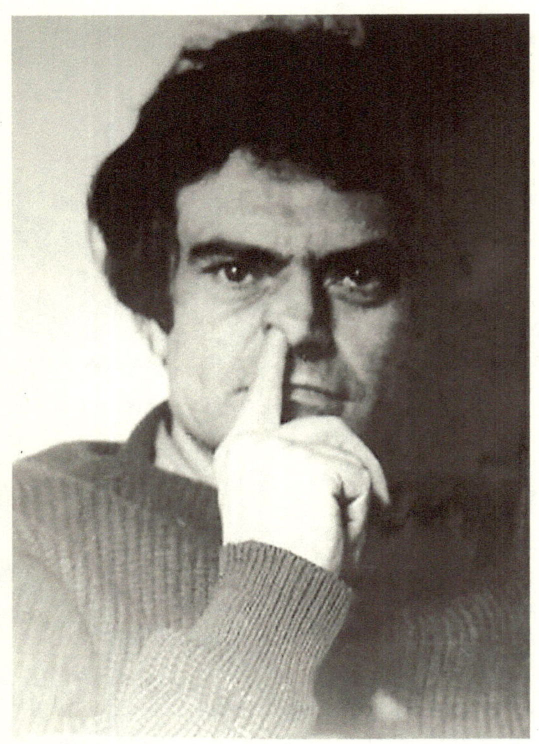

FIGURE 2.1
Portrait of Marcel Broodthaers in Action, date unknown, silver gelatin print on Leonar paper, 17.5 × 12.5 cm / 6.9 × 4.9 inches Photography by Maria Gilissen, © VG Bild-Kunst, Bonn 2016.

Manzoni orient themselves alike by means of that zero point of disorientation, the readymade: the liminal object that serves to mark symbolically the collapse of the difference between aesthetic value and value as such, the art object and the commodity.[5] Yet if Manzoni's fascinations turn on the seemingly infinite capacity of the spectator to imbue the artist with an illusionary substance, turning shit into gold, forcing the spectator to recognize that he or she can only plug up the hole in art's symbolic structure (the puncture wound of the readymade) by eating whatever shit the artist serves up, Broodthaers's approach is less derisory, less cynical, less confrontational; his focus lingers on the dereliction of being a thing that is, for better *and* worse, a creature of language.

Broodthaers's *rendez-vous* with Manzoni in which he was inscribed as a readymade seems in every way decisive: consigning his name to the status of an art object before its association with an artist-subject. He was astute enough to know that in designating him a readymade Manzoni had set a trap that he could only slip by identifying precisely with the nothing he had become. Rather than becoming the prop that elevated and secured Manzoni's identity, Broodthaers willingly accepted the test of being a readymade (that disjunct of a synthesis between shit and gold), acknowledging what he had become: a being separated from itself, without place, without name, an exile. A being, in short, that is not not-art. Identifying with the destitution of being an (art) object, internalizing the peculiar plight of being a readymade, that object forced out of its own mold, Broodthaers constantly staged and restaged the problem of becoming an artist, assuming this generic identity as a function of subjectivating the object he had become. An (art) object before being a(n) (artistic) subject, Broodthaers grasped that the problem of being an object is to make being a subject uneasy.[6]

****

Things that become readymades, objects of art, even if subjects (as in the case of Broodthaers), suffer a peculiar fate: the indignity of this fatal transport. If the readymade confers upon the artist, as Manzoni so lucidly discerned, a comically inflated dignity, the object nominated undergoes a pataphysical transformation in which its identity, while retained (a urinal remains a urinal), becomes irreparably altered (a urinal is no longer a urinal). The strangest of entities, the readymade is a thing that is not the thing that it is (a urinal) by being the very thing that it is (a urinal). Structurally insincere, the readymade presents itself sincerely as the thing it is not. Parsing the specificity of its non-sense requires shedding the conditioned response, as Broodthaers might say, of substituting the readymade's status (as art) for the enigma of its form: seeing not *that which* is given but merely the form of its givenness; that is, seeing nothing but the form of its conquest (the idea of the eagle).[7] The readymade is given as judged only if one agrees to see a urinal as a urinal, or conversely as not a urinal. However, the readymade marks the space given by the inclusive disjunction of both these judgments, in which a "collision" is staged between the identity of its form and the nonidentity of its place.

To see the readymade's form as the presentation of its absent place neither restores nor embraces its mythos of subversion. The enigma of its inscription as neither art nor not-art, its patalogical status, gets lost altogether in the mythos of its provocation, a subversive shock that quickly dissipates in the idiocy of those who simply ridicule it, the empty praise of those who seek to capitalize on a superficial negativity, or its neutral acceptance authorized by its place in the museum. Its patalogical status, however, cannot be effaced, precisely because its pataphysical status can only be produced as an event of carefully and calmly thinking through its patalogic.[8] The fear of its recuperation is really no fear at all, since what is recuperated never operates at the level of the problem it poses, but merely on the reception of its solution. The patience with which Duchamp carefully staged the "case of R. Mutt" is alone enough to disabuse us of such a notion.

The problem of the readymade becomes clearer if we approach it in terms not of what it does to art per se, but of what the readymade does to the object. Becoming a readymade, the object is stripped of the veil of sense provided either by its prosaic function (its use) or its arbitrary name, laying bare the null place its form occupies as not not-art. No longer serving to signify a use or place an identity, the readymade marks the nonidentity of its place. Having lost its name and its function, the readymade becomes a mute obstacle, a thing over which one can trip (*trébucher*),[9] designating the strange fact that significations are the trappings of things. Deprived of the illusion of being one with its name, the readymade's "indexical" meaning does not simply vanish; one still sees a urinal, a comb, a bottle rack. But as an *objet dard* these significations go limp; they no longer hit their mark. They no longer serve to rivet the form of the object to its signification. The loosening of their significations leaves the forms they designate as mere placeholders, no longer capable of imbuing their thingly matter with meaningful shape. Unbound from its signification, the form assumes a thingly presence locating the hole this form now makes in sense. The form presents a thing (lacking signification) that marks the place of an absence. In loosening the thing's relation to the form of its signification, the readymade becomes a mute signifier of this place, a figure of absence (fig. 0), that henceforth designates the null occupant of a hole in sense. This vacated place is the space of a displacement, making the form of the readymade an exhibit of the out-of-place. If this space is "lived unconsciously," as Broodthaers notes, by Mallarmé's typographic experiments in *A Throw of the Dice Never Abolishes Chance*,[10] with the readymade "space is really the fundamental element of artistic construction (form in language and material form)."[11] Yet what the readymade clarifies is the difference between the space of form (that which is displaced by form) and the form of space. Form thus conceals space as a structure of reification or a space of conquest, as Broodthaers often puts it, but space reveals form as the place of displacement: an *erewhon* stranger than paradise).

****

To take this thing that makes one stumble in earnest, i.e., to take it seriously as art, requires a *patalogical* sensibility. "*Arrhe* is to art [Earnest is to art]," Duchamp writes in the 1914 Box, "as shitte is to shit [*merdre est à merde*]."[12] Duchamp's allusion to Jarry's use of "*merdre*" in *Ubu Roi* is apt. To take the readymade in earnest is not to identify art with shit but with shitte (*merdre*). The senseless r (or *te* in its English rendering), whose addition can only be read, not heard, serves as a material differentiator: something that one cannot enunciate or pronounce, but that one can put one's finger on. The r is all too literally a stopgap, a wedge to stick into the crack, some *thing* to keep the door ajar. Treating the atoms of language like any other lump of senseless matter, Jarry wagers art on the possible "figuration" of a gap between nothingness and nothing, the undifferentiated and the indifferent. Pataphysics names the science of this senseless difference, this parsing of the void, that makes (all) the difference, making art possible as that measure of the measureless whose possibility Duchamp likens to a "*physical caustic*" that burns "up all aesthetics or callistics."[13] To bloat out this word with a senseless letter trades initially on the indiscernibility of shitte from shit for its crude effects. Jarry certainly had a penchant for scandal. Yet the sophistication of Jarry's *umour* (to allude to Jacques Vaché's notion to be expanded in the following chapter) lies in grasping the difference non-sense makes: a refinement that can only *appear* crude to one who lacks the means to measure it.[14] A urinal is just a crude object with a profane purpose, but R. Mutt's *Fountain* (1917), Duchamp's most Ubu-esque work, is pataphysical, making the readymade the atom of pataphysics and the artist who can conceive of it a patalogical thinker.

R. Mutt's courage—to the German ear R. Mutt passes seamlessly into *Armut*—is Ubuesque. It is the courage of the cretin and *Fountain* the most playful of monuments to stupidity and blindness. As Flaubert writes,

> Stupidity is immovable; nothing attacks it without shattering against it. It has the character of granite, hard and strong. In Alexandria, a Mr. Thompson of Sunderland wrote his name on Pompey's Pillar in letters six feet high. There is no way to see the pillar without seeing Thompson's name, and without consequently thinking of Thompson. The cretin has incorporated himself into the monument and perpetuates himself along with it.[15]

Unlike Mr. Thompson's graffiti that inscribes the insignificance of his name into a ruin of historical significance, Duchamp makes a monument of/to the insignificant by adding the bold letters of R. Mutt's name to a piece of plumbing. The "blind judges" of the Society of Independent Artists who received Richard Mutt's submission could see nothing other than error, a lapse of judgment, a category mistake whose unmistakable aim, they inferred, was to ridicule the very seriousness of their aims, missing the stupidity of *Fountain's* obdurate presence: the manner in which it thinks precisely through a logical *lapsus*, i.e., patalogically. Positioning art's visibility in relation to what cannot be seen problematizes in one stroke the blindness of the judge by confronting this allegorical figure with a figure of blindness. It will be the blind man, a figure who does not see what is before his eye, that will make possible an art positioned in its own blind spot: a nonretinal art.

The cretinism of the readymade is precisely a matter of being stupid like a painter (*bête comme un peintre*) to the point of substituting the stupidity of the act for the act itself. To become "stupid like a painter" is to become a dumb eye, an eye lacking thought, so the patalogician reasons: if the eye lacks thought, then to think from the position of that lack is to think an eye that does *not see* what it *thinks* it sees; if such an eye lacks vision, then a blind eye thinks only insofar as it sees its lack. Radicalizing Seurat's reduction of the subject to the retina that reduces the hand of the painter to a mere instrument of an eye that records the encounter with light—an eye "already encoded," as de Duve argues, "in the readymade discriminations provided by the paint manufacturer's color charts"[16]—Duchamp reduces the subject to the status of an impersonal encounter with the object. Duchamp identifies even more stringently with the impersonality of an aesthesis pushed to the point of indifference, abandoning touch and aesthetic discrimination altogether in favor of marking the blind spot that every retina contains. Such is the task of a nonretinal art and the patalogical reasoning it practices.

****

R. Mutt's *Fountain* is only registered as a historical event through the pages of a publication significantly titled *The Blindman*, put together anonymously by Duchamp with his friends Henri-Pierre Roché and Beatrice Wood to coincide with the Independents exhibition.[17] On the cover of the first issue, dated April 10, 1917, the day of the opening of the Independents exhibition, is a sketch by Alfred Frueh of a Chaplinesque blind man (a sort of Pierrot) being led through a painting exhibition by his dog. To see what is absent one must work like a dog. To work like a dog in French is *travailler comme une bête* (literally, like an animal). The figure sees with the dumb (*bêtise*) eyes of an animal (*bête*). Approaching poetry as a bestiary in *Pense-bête*, Broodthaers includes an entry on dogs: "The one my master has was remarkable. A real [*vrai*] blind dog."[18] To have an eye for stupidity (*bêtise*), to see its truth (*vrai*), one has to have an animal eye; one has to be blind to see what is given to an inhuman eye, that is, an eye not already coded by the human prejudices of the aesthete. And it is precisely such an inhuman eye, the eye of the camera, that records what was absent from the exhibition: "The Case of R. Mutt." Appearing at the end of the Independents with Duchamp's *Chocolate Grinder* on its cover, the second and last issue of *The Blindman* registers the event of *Fountain*'s quite literal absence from the exhibition. Soliciting Alfred Stieglitz's authority and formalist eye to document Duchamp's object, this issue carries his photograph of *Fountain* with the bold caption "THE EXHIBIT REFUSED BY THE INDEPENDENTS." It is *The Blindman* that lets one see the absent place of what was crudely kept from sight at the exhibition: *given but not shown*.

The title of the publication brilliantly slips along an associative chain: referring at once to the committee who rejected *Fountain*, "blind" jurors who

were "blinded" by its presence; the spectators visiting the exhibition, who were blind to *Fountain's* absence; and finally the position of the artist R. Mutt, a true blind dog that sees the nothing before his eyes. Only an artist who sees the void before him has an eye to see the possibility of art in the place of its absence, to propose a urinal as *Fountain*.

If one has to look at the readymade with a blind eye—or at least an eye profoundly lazy, an eye that is a bit slow, that lags behind—it is because concepts without intuition are blind, as Kant maintains. The readymade can only be seen from the position of such blindness, where the concept's application is at least momentarily delayed, where the impulsive judgment—this is not art—that conceptualizes the given *without delay* is suspended so that one can see (with an idiot eye) what is in fact given (to thought): the hole this intuition makes (in art) when its concept is absent. It is the one whose judgment is truly blind who sees what is given with the suspension of judgment: the mark of a blind spot, the null void of art's absent place, a blind intuition, a hole in sense marked by a lack of conceptual determinacy. Such a delay is necessary for the pataphysician to stutter: "Look! There is not … not art."[19]

A remarkable reversal takes place: the artist who holds onto the privilege of aesthetic form (the precedents of retinal art: painting, sculpture, etc.) becomes in the end a paltry logician. To test the blindness of the judge, one has to truly blindside him, or better, simply blind him with an object whose form of appearance blinds the judge at least long enough to sneak it into position, to place it in his blind spot. Making an object of this absence, the readymade positions the void, making palpable a patalogical hole in logic. Making an "art of logic" out of a logical *lapsus*, the patalogician allows us to see art's absence by thinking the logical peculiarity of its presence. Setting a logical trap that makes the eye trip over its form, the readymade delays the process of logical schematization, introducing the stutter: not not-art. The eye trips not because it sees but because it judges; it "sees" something that is not art (a urinal). But what makes it trip is not then *that which* it sees but *what* it sees (not art); and what it thinks it sees (not-art) is in fact a judgment (the relation given by the hyphen [-]). The readymade marks this difference between the given and the judged: the absent place of the not judged that digs a hole in vision with the senseless mark of the hyphen. One must see the absence to not fall for the trap. One can only trip, after all, over what one does not see. It is the blind man who will not trip over the readymade, because he sees its absence. Only as art does one see it—an it that is not a urinal nor a fountain, but a thing marking the vertiginous place where these vacated senses collide: a thing that is neither a urinal nor a fountain by being the null occupant of this disjunct (the space of a hyphen) that links these two names (urinal-fountain).

This space is not a matter of the making, but the placing. One can make art, but the space into which it must be placed is always (al)ready made. The readymade is not already made, but is made by what is displaced in the placing. In being placed, the readymade is "the figuration of a possible," which Duchamp conceives as neither "the opposite of impossible" nor given as a probability.[20] It only exists in the act of giving place to its absence. With the readymade Duchamp does not make art, but its possible place. In other words, he does not simply expose an object to the judgment "this is art." He marks its place as the possibility of its absence. The readymade thus figures its own absence: presenting itself as not-art to one who judges this absence, this "not," as present. What is present is not the judgment as such (the negation) but the place of the not (present absence). This subtle distinction between the relation to judgment and the place it marks is decisive to grasp the manner in which the readymade is a "figuration" of its absence, that is to say, the void it presents as its place. To become *anartist*, it is not enough to simply utter the judgment "this is art"; one must assume the place where this judgment is possible. If the possible, as Duchamp also maintains, is a "physical 'caustic' [vitriol type]" that dissolves the givenness of forms, the form's dissolution leaves a residue, stain, marking the given place of its possible absence.[21]

The inscription of the readymade, like adding an inaudible letter to *merde*, imperceptibly alters its form such that it acts as a physical caustic saturating the object, seeping into its pores as an "illuminating gas" that lights up its form as the gas eats away its content. Skinned, flayed, or stripped, the form remains as a sign of the thing's destitution. Its hollowed presence acts as a reminder, a *pense-bête*, of the difference between its figure (shape) and its signification. The figure's presence unbound from the constraint of its signification marks the outline of a hole in sense laid bare (splayed) by the pataphysical violence of the readymade's inscription (as art) that only comes into view when the eye is positioned in relation to what is not there (not art), seeing art in the very place of its absence. Like a mollusk torn from its shell, art becomes an amorphous anything whatever: inseparable from, while nonetheless indifferent to, the forms (*moules*) it assumes.[22]

The one who does not make art but who encounters its possible place (precisely where art is not) is what Duchamp named *anartist*. A nomination that patalogically includes its article in its determination by excising two letters, "ti" from anti-artist.[23] An artist not by making art but an object of its absence, anartist is neither an artist nor an anti-artist, but a contraction of this opposition that marks the visible but inaudible space between "an" and "artist": [an]artist. As an object compelled to exhibit its absence, anartist and the readymade make it possible to think the senseless place of art as the demarcation of a blind spot on the retina, the physical place of absent form. Able to see its own blindness because it thinks its own stupidity, this placer of art traces the path of a short circuit where non-sense is to sense as *arrhe* is to art, as *shitte* is to shit, as the nonretinal is to blindness, as *patologic* is to logic and pathology, as *anartist* is to an artist, as not not-art is to art, as the readymade is to form, as thing is to object, as the possible is to the impossible, as indifference is to the undifferentiated, as the I is to the me. The one who follows this circuit, as Duchamp suggests, "plays a game between 'I' and 'me.'"[24] Only a patalogical sensibility would presume the place of its absence, assuming the pataphysical space of art with deadly sincerity.

****

In 1960 in a series of works playing with and on his body as a site of pataphysical production, Manzoni probes the full extent to which the readymade and its "maker," anartist, stage a game between the I and the me. Shifting the readymade from the side of the object to the subject, Manzoni thinks the body of the artist as a possible site for the extraction of readymades. In *Artist's Breaths* from 1960, for example, Manzoni attaches a series of blown-up balloons to small wooden bases fitted with a plaque that reads: "Piero Manzoni—Artist's Breath." Treating the artist's own breath as a readymade, inscribing his own body into the space of production, the work becomes a travestied celebration of the artist's own dissipation. A work of diminishing returns, the orb's formal beauty sustained by "Manzoni's" physical presence slowly deflates, leaving its shriveled, inconsequential remains, an abject trace that presents the artist's absence. The deformation of the form of the balloon exhibits the dissipation of its subject-matter (artist's breath).

More than willing to exploit himself, the artist for Manzoni harnesses himself to value production, where the art object produced becomes the material bearer (as Marx describes the commodity's use value) of the idea. As Broodthaers would later recognize, Manzoni identifies "the commodity with the concept of the commodity," exposing the pretentions of conceptual art's vaunted immateriality *avant la lettre*. Manzoni's practice grotesquely parodies the fetishization of the commodity.

One of the enduring legacies of Marx's analysis of the fetish of commodities is to show that the abstract potency of capital's unrelenting expansion of the logic of exchange produces a "natural" illusion—a *belief* in the value of value. The notion of the value of value is sustained by the structural equivocation *and* contradiction between use and exchange value that acts as the motor of capital's expansionist logic and of its idealization. The constant confusion of quality and quantity, use and exchange, and their superimposition in the fetish is not an impediment, but the driving force that sustains and implicates the subject within the social field. It believes in the value of things, in the value of its world, in the value of itself. Capital does not prescribe a particular belief, but demands only *that* you believe. It is thus precisely the liquidation of all intrinsic value that becomes the condition of its continued production. Intrinsic value does not disappear, but appears to the subject as a thing in itself, withdrawn, a certain *je ne sais quoi* that essentially evades its grasp, a promise given as unfulfilled.

Manzoni assumes the place of art as such an empty promise: jokes at the audience's expense whose cynical punch lines are revelations of the slow wheeze of art's substance. In this grim scenario, the artist becomes a figure who plugs up the hole in value, the king of mussels (*moules*) whose absent presence is summoned to veil art's present absence. Often producing works designed to be consumed, hardboiled eggs baring his thumbprint (*Consumption of Art by an Art Devouring Public*, 1960), or products that can be sold but not consumed (*Artist's Shit*, 1961), Manzoni plays with the manner in which art as such, more specifically both its idea and its value, is produced as an effect of a social exchange inseparable from but irreducible to commodity exchange: the artist gives a part of himself and the collector gives his money. Agreeing to see art where it is not, the collector pays for something "worthless" and the artist gets something for nothing, his illusionary identity. Manzoni positions the place of the artist at a site of symbolic investment, making his patrons the all too willing victims of a confidence game in which less is substituted for more, nothing for something, shit for gold. Belief in his substance is the immaterial support of the art idea, and the all too material inscription of his signature. The artist becomes the willing prostitute of his idea, making the collector nothing but a john.

This confidence game is taken to the limit with *Declarations of Authenticity*, Manzoni's practice of designating "living persons" as artworks. To be "authenticated" by Manzoni as a work of art is to be the butt of a sophisticated *and* crude, but all ultimately cynical, joke. The living person becomes the unwitting victim of the artist's symbolic mandate: the staging of art as a structure of dialectical misrecognition in which there is nothing to be seen, but only a document to be read that contractually guarantees with a stroke of the pen that something did indeed take place as "art."[25] This nothing, which is merely staged symbolically as a signed declaration, serves to initiate a quintessentially narcissistic game in which "value" is produced as an empty reflection that makes the following empty promise: If you believe in my signature as the signature of an artist, then you will have been allowed by this king of mussels to see yourself infinitely reflected in my ephemeral substance. Believing in Manzoni allows you to trust in the integrity of his signature, which in turn allows you to see yourself *as a Manzoni*. Trapped in a narcissist's game, the victim of this becoming art, this becoming readymade, has no choice in the matter and must assume the subservient role of being a mere pawn, an animated prop, a slave, in the artist's game of mastery. And one can only assume one's role within the game (one's identity as artwork) if one recognizes the artist as master, as sovereign, as the "king of mussels," as Broodthaers later suggests.

Art becomes the tautological enterprise whose "integrity" depends on a belief in the value of the signature and the structures that authorize it and guarantee its authenticity. For Broodthaers to see himself, i.e., the person designated by the name, as a Manzoni is to recognize the structure of dependence between his readymade existence as art and the signature of its guarantee. The readymade becomes nothing other than a metonym for the artist's signature. Broodthaers becomes a Manzoni. This eclipse of the readymade's pataphysical surface and patalogical play allows for a cynical clarification: to see language's prosaic function and its institutional supports as the condition of art's (and therefore Broodthaers's) existence as art. Such conditions lay bare art's sociological existence, which makes of it the tarnish reflected in the imperium of the eagle's steely eye. To identify the idea of art with the figure of the eagle, which for Broodthaers "is exclusively a symbol of power, of ferocity,"[26] is to identify art and conquest, making it the apocalyptic décor of imperial order. Yet the artist is not, or at least for Broodthaers should not be, at home in this space that betrays the patalogical complexities of art. To be a Manzoni, to be anointed by this self-appointed sovereign, shows Broodthaers that the renewal of the patalogical place of art must entail an art that problematizes more than playfully enacts this position of mastery. If the person can in fact be an object of art (even if in name alone), a declaration that Broodthaers reads as a patalogical proposition, then the place of the artist, who is already an object of art, must assume the space of its displacement. Subject to art, the object-subject, Broodthaers, not one with himself, assumes the task of art as the division of the artist from his name, assuming the displacement of identity that the work entails. At odds with himself, the enemy of his own name, his own person, his own identity, Broodthaers assumes himself as a contradiction, assuming himself as compromised and insincere.

The artist is placed into the impossible position of having to betray himself in order to betray that betrayal: to be insincerely insincere. To be avant-garde, Broodthaers maintains, the artist must closely involve himself in "the commercial and marketing structure," in which theory itself plays a part, in order to produce the very effect of his symbolic existence as artist that he will henceforth have to distance himself from, problematize, interrogate, etc. For the artist to assume himself, his place within art and thus society, as a problematic site, he must assume the work as a deflationary site of the artist (rather than seeing the deflationary status of the work as an occasion for the potential resurrection of the figure of the artist).

When asked, for example, if he would include a Section Broodthaers in his "fictional museum," he responds:

> **MB:** No, no, no, no … not a Section Broodthaers. I'm not symbolic, I'm nothing.
> **MALE INTERVIEWER:** You're not part of a figure?
> **MB:** If you ask people who have already, people who know what I do, who have already seen my pictures, heard, seen things of mine, maybe I am some kind of figure for them. But I'm not even certain that when, you know, when I look at myself in the mirror, I am a figure. I'm not even sure that at the moment I represent a figure of an artist especially when I've shaved.
>
> Do you see what I mean?
>
> I think that the moment you take yourself for an artist when you look in the mirror, you think of yourself as a figure. And in fact, that is the difficult thing for an artist or a creative person in any field, not to see themselves as a figure, which I believe is the risk for a good many of us.[27]

With a humor at odds with Manzoni's sarcasm, Broodthaers proposes that we assume him as a fig. 0, observing the tortuous task in which his work serves to present him as absent. Accepting the artist as the tautological producer of "artistic" form, Broodthaers will work against the metonymic compulsion to simply substitute his name for the work, language for art. Not willing to identify himself as an "artist," he proposes perhaps that we think of him as not not an artist, a figure that did not, not choose to become an artist.[28]

****

Broodthaers's career as an artist begins with a declaration of insincerity; his declaration of his "artisthood" becomes an exercise in public relations. And it is with a now-infamous declaration of insincerity that he announced his first exhibition as an artist, which he had printed on folios taken from women's magazines:

> I, too wondered if I couldn't sell something and succeed in life. For quite a while I had been good for nothing. I am forty years old …
> The idea of inventing something insincere finally crossed my mind, and I set to work at once. At the end of three months I showed what I had produced to Philippe Edouard Toussaint, the owner of the Galerie Saint-Laurent.
> "But it is Art," he said, "and I shall willingly exhibit all of it."
> "Agreed," I replied. … If I sell something he takes 30%.
> It seems these are the usual conditions, some galleries take 75%.
> What is it? In fact, objects.[29]

The work, the objects, become the occasion of a complex staging of the artist's self-presentation, a *mise-en-scène* that serves to frame and unframe, introduce and obscure the place of the artist. The artist operates within the conditions of the market and is thus insincere, and yet he or she operates insincerely within the market. To become an artist, for Broodthaers, demands the full adoption of this constitutive insincerity. The artwork stages the disappearance of the subject only to make it reappear in a new guise and under new conditions, namely the conditions of artisthood. The suppression of the subject cannot do without a fiction of the subject. Repeatedly restaging the fiction of his "becoming an artist," Broodthaers makes the advent of art a complex staging ground for the presence and absence of a subject whose continued existence cannot be separated from the mechanisms that ensure its liquidation.

Broodthaers's first artwork and the central work of his first solo exhibition, *Pense-bête*, would be a hermetic allusion to his readymade identity. Encasing in plaster 50 volumes of his last book of poetry, also titled *Pense-bête*, Broodthaers appropriates *himself*, so to speak, as art object. Presenting his own poetry as art, he announces through "a public burial" a shift in identity from poet to artist. This shift is always plagued by a fundamental ambivalence, as much a radicalization of the position of the poet as that of the artist as merchandiser of the insincere. The trap of art, into which he stumbles, positions the subject in the place of its absence: marked, exposed as the void of the object.

To assume the artist function is to appropriate a structural loss of identity entailed by being an object, and this is what is put on exhibit with *Pense-bête*. Through metonymic substitution, *Pense-bête*, the work of art, takes the place of *Pense-bête*, the title of his book of poetry; at once a part and a whole, or, better, a part that names a whole, what is named by the name is precisely the gap that is figured, that space which is shown but escapes the name: the material difference that exposes the duplicity of the name. The duplicity of the name serves to mark the duplication of an identity: Marcel Broodthaers the poet, Marcel Broodthaers the artist. A book of poems become sculpture, *Pense-bête* stages art as the reminder (the most straightforward sense of the word *pense-bête*) of an absence, the exposure of the void, where an identity is formed through an act of displacement, substitution. The artist arises from the ruinous destitution of the poet.

Art becomes the practice of material inscription in which that which is named is paradoxically that which cannot be named but only shown: the object as zero word, as Broodthaers puts it. It is precisely the gap between showing and saying, between the multiplicity of the material given and the identity of the said, that makes it possible to think the duplicity of the name, the not-wholeness of the name, which draws our attention to the brute matter, the mute material, sitting there indifferently before the eye, at the very edge of language. Situating himself at the edge of language, at the very place where art and poetry meet through a parting of ways.[30]

Marking the outside of language on the inside of language, *Pense-bête* is a reminder of the stupidity at the origin of all thinking, that striving of a subject to think its own absence, which is left as a trace, like a fingerprint pressed into soft plaster.[31] A command to think (Think stupid! like Beckett's Think pig!) from the point in which identity itself can no longer provide orientation. To reach the animal on the inside of speech, the point of noncommunication, of "animal beauty," as he later puts it[32]—this is already the program of Broodthaers the poet. Within *Pense-bête*, the book of poetry, Broodthaers, the poet, proposes to think this form as the meeting point of contradictory figures: the space separating the mussel (*moule*) and the jellyfish (*méduse*).[33] Whereas the mussel (*moule*) is defined by its form (*moule*), by the shell that differentiates it from its background, turning it into a figure of "anti-sea" and allowing it to avoid "society's mould [*moule*]," the jellyfish is "Pas de moule" (not a mussel, not a mold or form) and thus "Rien que le corps" (Nothing but a body). These creatures are joined through their opposing relations to form. The jellyfish's non-form, or conversely the nothing (*Rien*) of its body's form, identifies its amorphous body with the repellent aspect of the mussel's shell: the material vacancy it traces. As mussels (*moule*) slip into their forms (*moules*) to become figures (separate from the background of the sea), the jellyfish (*méduse*) slips into its image, that of a medusa (*méduse*). The space between figure and image is traced by "sparkling words" whose marriage, that select pairing, produces an explosive figure (a "grenade") and images that turn words to stone (the hardening of their sense). The poem only touches on this space when sense gets lost: "when the vague outpouring wanders on [*ce crachement vague, vague*]." This last line on the page could be rendered thus: this surge of spit (like a wave) or this elusive spit surges (drools on). The page as a whole proceeds through breaking the tautology of word and sense: *moule/moule*, *méduse/méduse*, ending with the repetition, *vague, vague*. Positioning the word within the space where figure and image part reveals the blank stare of the page, whose gaze, like the medusa, turns the seeing eye to stone. And Broodthaers will later quote Baudelaire approvingly: "I am beautiful, O mortals, like a dream of stone."[34]

Broodthaers, the artist, would attribute the "shock that jolted [him] into producing works of [his] own" to an exhibition of George Segal's "mouldings."[35] In "Beware the Challenge!," a text from 1963, Broodthaers describes this work as "figurative art perhaps, but so stripped bare that it seems to fall into a special void."[36] By positioning plaster casts of human figures next to found objects, Segal's work only lays bare the difference between the object (a pinball machine, a squalid seat) and the subject (a figure cast in plaster) so as to expose their principled identity. Effacing the difference between the made and the readymade, the subject stripped bare becomes more object than the object, devoid of expressivity: "From Segal's characters we can find

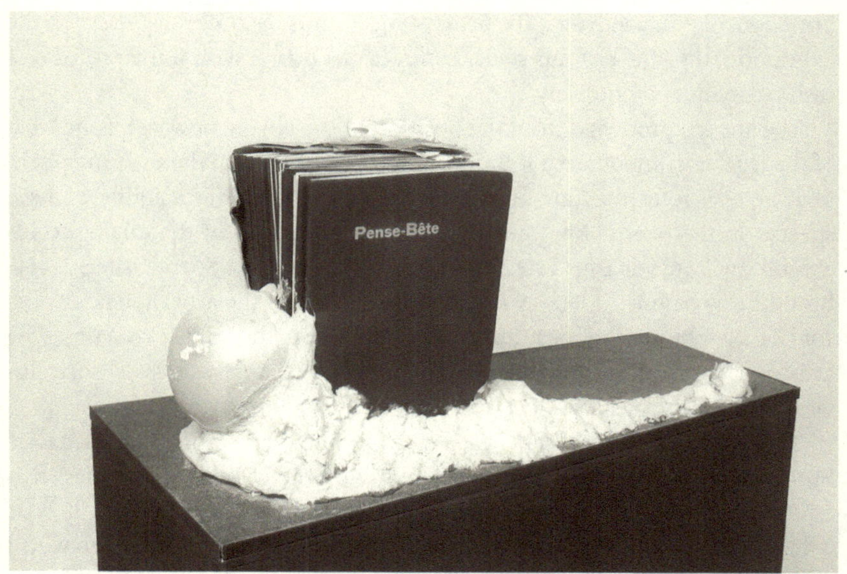

FIGURE 2.2

Marcel Broodthaers, *Pense-Bête*, 1964, books, paper, plaster, and plastic balls on wood base, 30 × 85 × 43 cm. © VG Bild-Kunst, Bonn 2016. Courtesy of S.M.A.K. Museum, Ghent. Photo by Dirk Pauwels.

out nothing."[37] The human stripped of its identifiable features becomes a "menacing" inhabitant of a "strangely lunar world." Confronted with this fundamental absence, this vacancy, the viewer, in this case Broodthaers, finds himself thrown back upon himself: "I could not write that they express terror without expressing my own."[38] Finding nothing with which to identify, the subject can only identify with its own lack of identity. One sees nothing but oneself in seeing nothing. "It's the victory of Narcissus. The humour is so black it blinds us."[39] Seeing nothing, one sees oneself as nothing: black humor indeed. In Segal, Broodthaers posits the exteriorization of all interiority, the self as a mere void, a mold (*moule*).

****

Broodthaers thus posits the artist as an object that speaks, a subject spoken by its becoming object. Becoming artist, the poet speaks from the position of the object. This is already suggested in the press release, quoted above in English translation, for his exhibition "Moi aussi, je me suis demandé ..." (I, too, wondered ...). The "me" (*moi*) precedes the question of "I" (*je*) that interrogates it as to its status, its social function. The merchant of the insincere is positioned through the object, and it is not Broodthaers himself but Toussaint, the gallerist, who declares the fruit of the "poet's" labor art. Not

not-choosing, Broodthaers, the artist-subject, thus becomes the effect of the exhibition, the effect of this social contract that brings with it the promise of cash payment and notoriety.

The speech produced from the position of the object, however, is not that of the legal document, even if Broodthaers does indeed, in the opening poem of *Pense-bête*, refer the "art of poetry" to the prosaic impossibility of legal speech. In the poem "My Rhetoric," which is included in the catalog to his exhibition "Mussels Eggs Fries Pots Coal" at Wide White Space Gallery, 1966, Broodthaers begins: "Me I say I Me I say I."[40] The I of the artist appears as the void of the object (the me), just as the shell traces the void it contains. The artist is always already an object before being a subject: this *material* sociolinguistic fact is the obstacle over which any artistic subjectivity trips.

This is what Broodthaers learned from the *rendez-vous* with Manzoni. Broodthaers took this comical act *in earnest* with the genuine seriousness that a *pataphysical* truth deserves, working out its *patalogical* implications. It is as if he said to himself: Insofar as I am a work of art, I am no longer who I took myself to be: *no longer* a poet, but *not yet* an artist. The act of becoming a readymade entailed the suspension of his prior identity, and Broodthaers understood that in order for him (the subject) to come to know who he had become (Broodthaers the art object), he had to come to terms with the hyphenation of his identity (no longer a poet, not yet an artist). If I insist on this strange formula of becoming artist, it is because through this hyphenation Broodthaers poses the problem of artistic subjectivity as inseparable from the conditions that pertain to the *act* of exhibiting, making the exhibition that stage where this alien identity is navigated.

The exhibition itself becomes a stage where Broodthaers appropriates his own objecthood through the hyphenation that suspends the identity of the artist between the poles of his or her individual becoming. The presentation of the hyphen is only possible through the act of exhibiting: where the identity of the artist is substituted for an object that marks the void of his place. The objects on exhibition become attached to a name, Broodthaers, that becomes the name of an *artist*: a poet impersonating an artist. A subject wagered on the nonsensical excess of a name—all those extra signifiers that signify nothing, that can be seen but not heard littering his name: Broodthaers, not *Brotars*.[41]

Committing himself to the whim called art, to this "cemetery without hope,"[42] he makes a narcissistic wager investing in the non-sensical excess of the name, those useless letters that become the armor of one's signature.[43] The "curse of the artist," he says on the occasion *Un jardin d'hiver* (1974), is to be identified with "what he does. In fact people say, collectors say, 'Yes, I have three what's-his-names on this wall, or four what's-his-names,' the way one says, 'I have two cars, shares'—isn't that it? Generally speaking, my name is difficult to pronounce and so I think I escape that fate a little. I am called Marcel Broodthaers."[44] If art is unable to trouble the ease with which one pronounces its name, making the tongue trip over a letter or the eye over an absence, it becomes mere décor. Broodthaers, however, never gives up on art's patalogical vocation: learning to speak the language of meows or substituting the eyes of a camel for those of the eagle. Bringing humor to one's destitution, or perhaps one should say umour, art—like an egg without a yoke—is a black sun that positions the artist in the space of its very absence.

CHAPTER 3

A SENSE OF UMOUR: JACQUES VACHÉ

Like the sketches of dandified officers and gentlemen that populated the margins of his wartime letters, Jacques Vaché seems at once the object of refined construction and a thing haphazardly dashed off, a meticulously rendered doodle exhibiting an ease and composure ruefully out of step with the horror of his circumstances: the harsh reality of trench warfare in World War I. Whether portraying himself or his surrogates (gentlemen portraits of André Gide's Lafcadio),[1] he sketches the outline of a stylized monstrosity: a dandy at the front, a figure whose subjectivity can only be traced by means of an abstract line, elegant and meandering, whose trajectory charts the wandering course of an absence. A subject that *deserts itself from within*—to paraphrase Breton's apt formula to describe Vaché's singular mode of self-relation, his resumption of the dandy's taste for treating his subject as a thing among objects. It was the gruesome backdrop of the war with all its grim stupidity that lent to Vaché's dandyism the affect of deadpan humor—a strangeness of tone that he himself would mark by an absence that could be seen, that is, *read*, but not heard: umour.

Umour bears a relation of course to humor, without which it could and would not be. But this relation occasions something irreducible to that relation, the advent of a subject that occupies the null place of this excised h and is charged with maintaining a difference that is perilous and threatened with loss—a subject with a sense of umour. Umour is less a thing that can be referred to, or a sense that can be defined, than an operation (a countersense) that expropriates sense, not simply the sense of humor but sense as such, through this particular act of excision: umour cuts itself off from humor. And Vaché's genius lies in what quite easily could be passed over merely as a bad joke, a bit of stupidity: a mere misspelling. But this bad joke, this bit of silliness, this error, if approached with the requisite seriousness, founds an operation whose effect produces a concept (or is it an

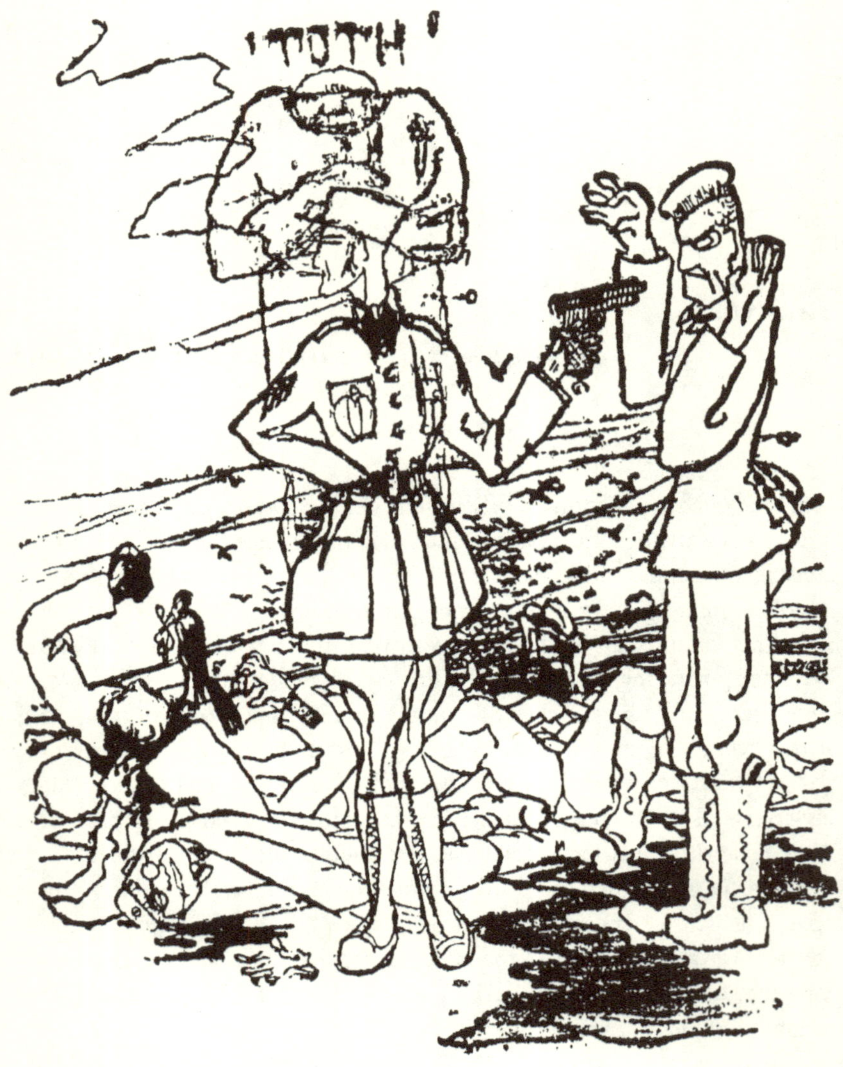

FIGURE 3.1
Self-portrait by Jacques Vaché, as it appeared in *Lettres de guerre* (Paris: au Sans pareil, 1919).

anticoncept?)—umour—and a subject that is engendered in the act that thinks it. Thus we have two moments: the excision of the word whose concept, in turn, induces the excision of the person. The subject of umour is not a person, which is to say a subject that installs itself in the gap between the I and the me, making Vaché the impersonator of his own nullity.

Vaché's descriptions of umour are often evasive and even surreal *avant la lettre*: "you know the horrible life of the alarm clock—it's a monster that has always frightened me because of the number of things its eyes project, and the way in which this honest man stares at me whenever I enter a room—why then does he have so much 'umour, why?"[2] But he is at his least evasive when he writes: "There is a lot of wonderful UBIQUE in 'umour also—as you will see—But—of course, this isn't definite and 'umour derives too much from a sensation of not being very difficult to express—I think that it's a sensation—I was going to say SENSE—also—of the theatrical (and joyless) futility of everything."[3]

If umour is a matter of a lapse or a failure (a bit of idiocy) or absentmindedness—and Vaché tells us, alluding to Jarry's Ubu, that it is wonderfully UBIQUE—it nonetheless more closely approaches the sense of humor by way of its missing part than does humor itself—that is to say the word. The sense of humor is humorous, but humor (the word) is not literally humorous. And this gap between word and its sense (what it means) is constitutive of the word's reference. Whereas humor is not humorous, umour perhaps becomes so, and increasingly, the more it is insisted upon: the more its difference from humor is insisted upon. For one of the few responses that Vaché gives to Breton's request for a definition of umour is: "IT IS IN THE ESSENCE OF SYMBOLS TO BE SYMBOLIC."[4] Whereas humor, the word (the signifier), cannot refer to itself as an instance of humorousness, umour is that which it is not: it is humorous. Humor excludes its sense; umour includes its sense. It is identical to that which it is not. And its sense derives from this vacuity: a word whose sense is in turn indexed to the absent place of the letter (the missing h). Umour (due to the excision) is not humor, but in being not-humor it can be literally humorous. Through the inclusion of this negation as its content, it enacts its own vacancy and it becomes the thing that it is not. As humorous, it is itself by being not-itself, performing the thing that humor (the word) cannot.

We have a material differentiation (at the level of the signifier) that produces an apparent superposition of sense: humor, a sense referred to; and umour, a sense produced through negation. This superposition is misleading. The humorousness of umour derives from either its stupidity or its playfulness. It does not share humor's "goodness," which is exposed by the idiom in English: "Will you humor me?" Humor is bound up with "good will." Umour, on the contrary, is inseparable from a maliciousness, an ill will, trespass and violence—all of what Deleuze associates with misosophy[5] and Breton with "black humor." Umour is essentially improper. To have a sense of umour is to have a sense for the (joyless) futility of sense—its vacuity.

****

We have looked at the way in which umour is a sense, but how is it a sensation? Vaché's appropriation of this absence, his adoption of a misspelling, sets into motion a comical play between the act of saying (speech) and the inscription of the said (written language). The I solicited to enunciate the word "umour" can only acknowledge that which is amiss in it by remaining silent, by not saying but recording what is said *literally*. I must perform this absence by not speaking. As soon as I say "umour," I betray it. To literally record the phonic pronunciation excises the *h*, cleaving the sensation from the garment of sense. One hears correctly, that is, literally, but transcribes incorrectly; one writes down umour instead of humor. One acts *as* if one did not know the language that one speaks. One has to become an unconscious recorder, a true mime. Literalization forces an estrangement between the word and its sense. And this *as if* introduces a foreignness, a silent and insidious incursion, into the language one speaks. Umour produces a short circuit between sensation and sense, that which is registered, recorded, transcribed and that which is understood. Umour exposes that sense implies a disavowal of the literal and that this disavowal makes possible understanding. To transcribe knowingly entails that one understands in advance that humor includes a silent *h* such that when one says umour one means humor. Vaché's insistence on the excision entails a perversion of this aim—as if one could say humor but *mean* umour, twisting it by means of an ill will. Umour cannot be said but only done, enacted; it has to be spelled out. If it is uttered, enunciated, spoken, its effect cannot be felt on the word, but only on language as a whole when enacted as silent, material excision. As such, umour situates the subject called upon to enunciate it in the gap between sensation and sense, a gap moreover that threatens the sense of the word with the non-sense of its articulation, instituting an asymmetrical (nonoppositional) break between sense and non-sense. Non-sense distinguishes itself from sense, but sense does not distinguish itself from non-sense. Deleuze calls this a "unilateral distinction"; its material difference has to be affirmed. It is this difference that makes a difference insofar as its sense now entails non-sense. Umour is both a sensation and a sense of the futility of making sense. By implication: If the sense of umour is humorous, then that which is humorous in umour is non-sense. Umour names a non-sensical sense or a sense of the non-sensical.

There is something comical as well about the fact that umour's sense (its meaning) cannot be uttered, that its sense can only be sensed. When one says "umour," its very utterance conceals the fact that it is amiss, that anything is awry (a parody perhaps of the ubiquitous insistence on troop morale)—its sense appears to be the same, but all the while it has been corrupted by an absence, an absentee letter whose failure to appear marks the word deviously, directing it off course, as if to amplify its own silence. It both obeys and refuses the laws of sense in being misheard, and it plays rather a game with the sense of humor that threatens it with its own non-sense of a senseless excision. The sonic equivalence of humor and umour reduces the sense of umour to humor in order force a counter reduction that renders its sense equivalent to non-sense. Its non-sense cannot be said but only sensed as the very gap between sense and sensation. As such, umour cannot be communicated; it can only be performed or enacted. Or, paradoxically, it is a sense that derives from not being understood. As a word it fails at the level of sense, while differentiating itself at the level of language's brute matter. It conveys its own senseless noise in the form of a resounding silence.

****

If one follows, as I have attempted to do, this paradoxical logic of umour, one grasps that its power consists in this *principled* reduction: the reduction of sense to non-sense. If it did not take us too far afield, it would be interesting to pursue how this reduction is a comical parody of the phenomenological reduction. Although umour performs the operation of this reduction to non-sense in an exemplary manner by exposing this gap between sensation and sense, each word can in turn be estranged through its reduction to its materiality. Non-sense, far from being excluded from sense, establishes itself as the null sovereign of its own enterprise afflicting language as a whole. Umour marks a gap in sense, a non-sense, that threatens all sense with the vertigo of its own vacancy.

The operation of umour is twofold: it reduces sense to sensation (through an act of literal inscription), i.e., to the gap between sensation and sense, and thereby separates sense from its content. It evacuates sense, it liquidates it. All sense is potentially non-sensical. As an operation, umour is at once material and formal, and it is this duality that inflects Vaché's dandyism, giving it theoretical teeth. Paul Lenti writes, "As a product of this new century, Vaché saw reality itself as a game; it was all a question of style. He often fantasized about major deceptions while he indulged in such pranks as introducing himself and others under false names, wearing a variety of disguises, bragging about invented pasts, etc."[6] Umour does not restrict itself to the word but propagates itself as a sensibility that relates to itself and language through this gap between sensation and sense, through which all sense can be rendered non-sensical. Vaché the subject becomes the differentiator of this difference between the sense of umour and humor. And it is this difference that gives definition to Vaché's attitude, expressed as much in his official capacities as in his writing:

> [to Breton] I'm the English interpreter, a position to which I bring a total indifference decorated with a quiet farce—such as I like to bring to official things—I take my Crystal monocle and a theory for troubling paintings for a walk around villages in ruins.

> I've been successively a crowned man of letters, a well-known pornographic artist, and a scandalous cubist painter—Now, I stay at home and leave the task of explaining and discussing my personality to others.[7]

If this passage is umourous, its locus lies in the question of whom Vaché takes for a walk. Although it is his superiors in his official capacity whom he formally addresses, whom he actually addresses is his "Crystal monocle" and his "theory for troubling paintings." And by addressing these "objects" that ornament his subject, he separates himself from this official role while performing it, producing a *personal* effect that is not his concern, that is, not the concern of his subject. If we can conceive of Officialdom as a structure that requires that one appear in person and be accountable, Vaché is only present through his personal effects that serve to occasion an absence, the flight of his consistent identity.

Umour attunes Vaché to the secret action of language's materiality, a materiality that does not simply undermine the subject that speaks but serves as its armature and ornament: the means through which Vaché installs himself perilously in the gap between his subject and his person. Vaché looks at words through the magnifying glass of his crystal monocle. Words, like clothes, become ornamentation that empties out the self as if it were a mold (*moule*). Umour lends a singular tone that proliferates across Vaché's letters. For example, if descriptive, he is generally laconic, even to a comic degree: "I'm bored a lot behind my glass monocle, I dress in khaki and fight the Germans."[8] In general the writing is oddly neither literary nor exactly casual in tone, as if at once whimsical and highly considered. His profligate use of the dash, furthermore, hacks his language apart, imbuing it with a sense of incompleteness and his thoughts with an impulsive, capricious punctuality: (to Breton) "Remember that I like you a lot (and you must believe this)—and that I would kill you moreover—(without scruples, perhaps)—after first having rifled you of unlikely possibilities."[9] When funny, the tone is dark and macabre: "I hope this document reaches you while you are still alive and doubtless keeping busy cutting off arms and legs with a saw, according to tradition, and wearing a nice white apron on which a hand leaves greasy prints in blood."[10] Aloof, sartorial, and corrosive, the I that is omnipresent seems unhinged but lucid, as if maintaining itself at the edge of delirium: "I dream of nicely felt Eccentricities or of some droll deceit that causes a lot of deaths, all in a very light molded costume; sporting. Can you show me beautiful shoes, open and garnet-colored?";[11] or, "I will also be a trapper, or thief, or prospector, or hunter, or miner, or oil-driller—Arizona Bar (whisky—Gin and mixed?), and lovely exploitable forests and you know those lovely riding breeches that you wear when using a machine-gun, clean-shaven and such lovely hands for solitaire. All that will go up in smoke, I tell you, or, in a saloon, having made a fortune—*Well*."[12]

From such passages in which the I is staged as grandiose and absurd, one can grasp why Breton—whose admiration for Vaché never wavered—writes: "In Vaché's person, in utmost secrecy, a principle of total insubordination was undermining the world, reducing everything that seemed all-important to a petty scale.'"[13] Yet this staging of the I breaks with romanticism insofar as it goes hand in hand with an utter deflation of the self. Breton expands on this principle in his introduction to Vaché in the *Anthology of Black Humor*:

> His refusal to participate is absolute, and takes the guise of a purely formal acceptance pushed to the limit: he maintains all the "outer signs of respect," of a somewhat automatic acquiescence to precisely what the mind deems most insane. With Jacques Vaché, not a cry, not even a whisper: man's "duties," which were typified in the agitation of those times by "patriotic duty," are defied—up to and including conscientious objection, which in his view still showed far too much good will. In order to find the desire and the strength for opposition, one still needs to fall less short of the mark. Instead of outward desertion [*désertion à l'extérieur*] in time of war, which for him still retained a rather *Palcontent* aspect, Vaché opted for another kind of insubordination, which we might call desertion within oneself [*la désertion à l'intérieur de soi-même*, which could be rendered more literally as desertion of the interior of the self].[14]

If the self or the person—whose equation we first owe to John Locke—is the seat of moral responsibility, Vaché's desertion divests the subject of its belief in the self. From the excision of the letter to that of the subject, umour provides him a means of pursuing a *principled* anarchy. He becomes an absentee subject. To be absentee is a matter of being marked absent. Whereas a delinquent is marked absent by a teacher, and thereby held to account, Vaché preemptively absents his *self*. He marks himself absent by separating himself from that which holds him to account, actively assuming the void of his presence.

The uncanny effect of this excision makes Vaché not a person, but an impersonator of a subject. The impersonator divests the self, the person, of its obligation to appear identically, which is why the impersonator has always proved such a troubling figure. Impersonation poses the problem of the identity or nonidentity of the subject with its manner, the grain of the voice, the sweep of its gesture. At once producer and produced, the self of the imitator is split, divided in two: itself only by being not itself. Only insofar as the subject is not bound singularly to its manner can that manner be imitated, impersonated, caricatured. As Plato recognized, to produce an imitation of the soul requires a soul that is itself protean, capable of separating itself from itself. To impersonate is to don the mask (the *persona*) of the other. But in becoming other, the imitator becomes other to itself. And it is precisely this negation that is registered with the *im* of impersonation. To impersonate implies a negation of who one is, assuming the character of who one is not. A duplication of the self by itself.

Impersonation is not merely the assumption of a false identity but the disavowal of a "true" identity. In putting forth an identity, the impersonator does not believe in that identity; he does not think he is that which he appears to be. Insofar as the impersonator says "I," this saying is insincere. For the I that speaks is not attributable to the self, but to the me that appears—not the subject but the person. The impersonator asserts as a matter of practice that the I is never where it appears to be. Like the lion in *A Midsummer Night's Dream*, the impersonator can state: "I am the lion, and I am not the lion, but Snug." The impersonator plays with this gap between the I and the me, forging an identity that eludes a determinate grasp, shifting perpetually from the position of the subject to that of the object, as if saying "the lion is *me*, but I am Snug." The I of the impersonator is fatally split (I am and I am not who I say I am) and can only be mediated through an act that assigns it a proper name. The proper name allows the opposition to be attributed to a subject that mediates the gap between the I and the me, enabling a me to designate an I. But what is the foundation of the *propriety* of the name? If the impersonator is true to who he is, then the very propriety of this name is in question, just as Andy Kaufman can state, "Andy Kaufman is me; I am Andy Kaufman." The name is the mask of impropriety. Andy Kaufman's insistence on being both I and me becomes rather an homage to a nameless subject without propriety.

Impersonation remains good fun—*in good humor*—as long as the difference between the person and the subject can be measured, discerned. If this measure vanishes, if impersonation slips into imposture, the playful becomes deranged. The key to Vaché's umour is its dryness, his capacity to deadpan. This is the core of his dandyism: to be absent but not to acknowledge one's absence, or to believe enough in one's absence not to get sentimental. It is deadpan that gives dandyism both a comical and a deathly edge.

****

Although Vaché acknowledged Charlie Chaplin, Buster Keaton's manner may be closer to umour. The portmanteau word "deadpan" was coined by a critic from the *New York Times* to describe Buster Keaton's singular manner of playing it straight, a lesson that he learned early in the vaudevillian slapstick of The Three Keatons in which he performed with his father, Joe, and his mother, Myrna, as The Human Mop. As he would later comment, "the more seriously I took everything, and how serious life was in general, the better laughs I got." "One of the first things I noticed was that whenever I smiled or let the audience suspect how much I was enjoying myself they didn't seem to laugh as much as usual. ... At any rate it was on purpose that I started looking miserable, humiliated, hounded, and haunted, bedeviled, bewildered, and at my wit's end. Some other comedians can get away with laughing at their own gags. Not me."[15] To deadpan consists in neither identifying nor acknowledging the effect one has on the other and thereby on oneself. To deadpan consists in blinding one's self to the manner in which one is perceived, and it is this lapsus itself, this incongruity, that produces a laugh. Again commenting on his early comedic training, as reported by his biographer, Rudi Blesh: "The old man would kick me, a hell of a wallop with a number twelve slapshoe right on my fanny. … Now a strange thing developed. If I yelled ouch—no laughs. If I deadpanned it and didn't yell—no laughs. "What goes?" I asked. "Isn't a kick funny?" "Not by itself it ain't," said Joe. So he gives me a little lesson: I wait five seconds—count up to ten slow—grab the seat of my pants, holler bloody murder, and the audience is rolling in the aisles. I don't know what the thunder they figured. Maybe that it took five seconds for a kick to travel from my fanny to my brain. Actually, I guess, it was The Slow Thinker. Audiences love The Slow Thinker."[16] Slow thinking is funny; full retardation is not. If one is an entertainer, this is a limit one does not want to cross. However, umour consists in refusing the moment of shared knowledge, of mutual recognition that serves to release the tension, the unease. Whereas humor offers the promise of release, umour maintains itself in this gap, this interval or delay. For although humor inserts a delay between cause and effect—between the kick and hollering bloody murder—it is umour that puts into question the causal relation as such. The slow thinker slows the relation between A and B, action and reaction; the umourist plays the idiot, dislocating the subject who acts and the self that is affected (the I that receives the kick and the self that feels it), refusing to identify with the manner in which he becomes an object for the audience, the manner in which he is perceived. He is out of step with himself, not keyed into the manner in which he affects the audience: dumb and aloof.

The mature and masterful Keaton focused this tension on the monumental impassivity of his own face. Where we expect some kind of human reaction, we get nothing. If the face is generally used to establish intimacy, enabling empathy between the viewer and the character's emotional state, Keaton's refusal of empathy situates his character outside of the range of expected feeling. Hence his distaste for the close-up. This is comedy at its least sentimental, at its least empathic. It short-circuits what David Hume has described as the "universal tendency among mankind to conceive all beings like themselves." Now whereas we doubtless identify Keaton's face as human, recognizing in it a shared physiognomy, its impassivity interrupts the *prosopoietic* operation by which humans "transfer to every object, those qualities with which they are familiarly acquainted, and of which they are intimately conscious."[17] Rather than finding a human face in the disposition of stone, we find in a human face the disposition of stone. Its featurelessness resists the ascription to it of a shared *humanity*. It looks human, but is it human?

Keaton's face serves rather to establish a radical distance, an essential non-relation between Keaton and the emotional reactions that enable identification. No longer a person to be identified with, he becomes an object to be laughed at. Unaffected by the turmoil in which he finds himself entangled, he acts without reacting. The chaos surrounding him engenders a strange neutrality, distanced not only from the circumstances in which he is embroiled but from the self affected thereby. It is an estrangement absolute, a face that has become a pure, inscrutable surface into which nothing can be read. He cannot be undermined, because there is nothing to mine. Deadpan quite literally describes the deadness of Keaton's face—a face-skull expressionless like bone. He is an object, his visage delivered up to the gaze of others, but in what sense is he a subject? What is laid bare in the lifelessness of his expression?

****

Through deadpan Vaché constitutes himself as subject without personality. Put differently, his character constitutes itself as a subject that is not a person. His persona does not serve to conceal his identity, but his identity consists in not identifying with his persona. In this face, we discern a human stripped of its humanity. In becoming a pure face, a face without expression, reduced to being a face-thing, it becomes simply a surface for the other without interiority. As an object it hides something else right on its surface, for its very objectness is that which cannot be reflected, for the other that would reflect it cannot see itself confirmed in this surface. Deadpan exposes the impersonality of the face. It is in this sense that he becomes an object for the other. He becomes an object only by suspending the signs that would allow the other to discern in the face a personality, an interiority, a depth. The inscrutability of Keaton's face becomes an object that interrupts the circuit of its recognition. But this other can no longer discern in the face anything that would allow it to ascribe to it anything personal. By becoming inscrutable the face becomes impersonal, inhabited by an alien subjectivity but not a person. With this deadpan reduction Keaton effects a split between his personhood and his subjectivity. He becomes a subject without being a person. An absentee subject that marks its absence through the suspension of its personhood.

Vaché seemed to have excised in himself that belief—that need for belief—that seemed so necessary to the subject's social inscription, discarding the proprietary relation that one has with one's self. In so doing, he pinpoints a certain slippage between property and propriety (ownness) whereby personhood, the self, is not viewed as an ontological matter—something that is—but as something that one *has*. Vaché *owned* his radical lack of significance, embracing the accidental quality of existence, forging his own brand of gay science: umour, or, the practice of excising significance from existence.

Vaché fictioned for himself a life truly elsewhere and an I that is other. For those who appreciated his singular existential cadence (André Breton above all), Vaché was a subject who had truly absorbed the nihilistic lesson of the times: "Jacques Vaché," Breton writes, "was a past master in the art of 'attaching little to no importance to anything.'"[18] His death of an opium overdose at the age of 23 shortly after the war in 1919—a suicide? accident, or perhaps both?—completes the picture: as Breton put it, "His death was admirable in that it could pass for an accident."[19] Necessarily accidental, a final excision that at once means everything and nothing.

CHAPTER 4

THE RIDICULOUS SUBJECT

Near the end of his life, on his nightly visit to his friend Dr. Saltas, Alfred Jarry could be seen "dressed in furs and shod in slippers" with "a heavy leaded cane" and "flanked with two pistols," of course.[1] In stories told about Jarry, it is not simply the fact of the pistol but its presence *of course—the "unshakeable alliance between Jarry and the pistol"*[2]—that makes it the conduit of his darkest humor. It is not the object per se but Jarry's relation to it that makes it something both menacing and hilarious, serving, as André Breton suggests, as the "the final key to his thought."[3] Attached to Jarry's person, the pistol becomes a pure affectation, an event that hollows the person of Jarry as it empties the pistol of its substance. The pistol punctuates his stride, alters the course of his gait, becoming a matter of comic timing and acting as a kind of calling card announcing the fiction of Jarry's presence. Jarry does not simply disarm the pistol, but through Jarry the pistol becomes something disarming: altering not only the object (the pistol) but also the subject (Jarry). The pistol becomes a rhetorical device, whose senseless outbursts lend Jarry's voice, as André Gide suggests in *The Counterfeiters*, a mechanical air: "that toneless voice of his—a voice without warmth or intonation, or accent or emphasis."[4] In Jarry's hand, the gun loses its menace, exuding a delinquent humor, becoming a senseless amusement, a means to uncork a few bottles of champagne.[5] As if inserted into an alternative logic, the pistol loses its gravitas while the person loses its grip. Jarry's attachment to the pistol marks the advent of *Jarry* the artist: not the person, but the name J-a-r-r-y signifying the effect of this encounter.

Is it Jarry that subverts the pistol by playing with and against its manufactured ends, or is it the pistol that perverts Jarry, compelling him to deviate from the norms that would regulate its use? The question is moot. It marks a site of displacement. The pistol becomes, as Breton writes, "the paradoxical hyphen between the outer and inner worlds."[6] Such that when we mention

Jarry, we should add: *he who pistols*.[7] Hyphenating Jarry's identity, the pistol becomes a ridiculous object, a violently comical *act* that stands in for the person of Jarry: making *him* he who *pistols*. Having lost the seriousness of its form, the pistol becomes for Jarry a surrogate, a theatrical accoutrement, a mask, announcing the presence of an absence, serving as a kind of cane that accentuates a limp, supporting him in his *unbelief*, as if propping up a dissolute identity. It *acts* him, and Jarry becomes a grotesque caricature of the pistol: an utterly ridiculous subject.

Jarry's pistol in all its hyperbole renders manifest the indignity of being an object. That is to say, a thing at best condemned to signification, to meaning, to sense, and at worst condemned to being the paltry servant of man. The thing's elevation through language, like the posing subject's cock of the chin, lends it an affected manner that Jarry exposes by becoming the pistol's comical event.

****

As its etymology attests, from the Latin *ridiculosus*, the ridiculous is bound up with the laughable. Manifest in that which is out of place, the peculiar, the odd, the incongruous, the awkward, and all that lacks conformity, in the malformed or the deformed, the non-sensical and the absurd, that which is ridiculous suffers from an often sudden depreciation, a loss of value, or a lack in logical form, as in *reductio ad ridiculum*. Laying bare a void in the structural order of things or a deformation of an object's appearance, the ridiculous punctuates the reduction to nothing of something with a burst of laughter, that uneasy discharge that signals that something is awry.

Signaling a loss of propriety, a lack of seriousness, the ridiculous appears as a discrepancy between the form of an appearance and its manner. Manners, as taught in handbooks for the maintenance of decorum, can be defined as the art of appearing non-ridiculous, of maintaining accord between an act and its signification. And it is this relation to the form of seriousness that lends their prescriptions a ridiculous air. A book like Erasmus's *On Good Manners for Boys* now appears all the more ridiculous for the seriousness of its tone. It becomes ridiculous the more it appears to insist on its seriousness. Take the following example:

> Thus, for the well-ordered mind of a boy to be universally manifested—and it is most strongly manifested in the face—the eyes should be calm, respectful, and steady: not grim, which is a mark of truculence; not shameless, the hallmark of insolence; not darting and rolling, a feature of insanity; nor furtive, like those of suspects and plotters of treachery; nor gaping like those [of] idiots; nor should the eyes be constantly blinking, a mark of the fickle; nor gaping as in astonishment—a characteristic observed in Socrates; not too narrowed, a sign of bad temper; nor bold and inquisitive,

which indicates impertinence; but such as reflects a mind composed, respectful, and friendly. For it is no chance saying of the ancient sages that the seat of the soul is in the eyes.[8]

Manner marks the externalization of the internal; in Erasmus's terms, the sensible manifestation of the mind. The ordering of the sensible appearance is structured according to the establishment of a rule that assigns propriety of place to that which appears, lending sense to the eye's various movements. Like style in dress, which should be in "accord," according to Erasmus, with one's "means and station" and one's "locality and its standards,"[9] the meaning of the eye's movement is structured according to a series of differences (calm, respectful, and steady versus grim, insolent, and shameless) that situate the eye within a gap between its appearance and its formal (normative) determination and whose relation constitutes manner. The eliminability of this gap, the failure of a form to adequately establish conformity between what appears and its manner or guise, creates the space for ridicule. If the ridiculous is that which is without place, ridicule as the art of derision locates the place of the out-of-place.

The ridiculous is thus an irruption of negativity that registers the impropriety of that which appears. And this impropriety can be manifest through either an excess of form (a mannerism) or a lack of form (the formless). If the latter produces horror, it is the former that produces laughter whose absolute form, according to Baudelaire, is the grotesque. In either case, it is symptomatic of a loss of grace: the comical effect of the separation of something from its manner. As Kleist writes in "On the Marionette Theater," such separation appears as affectation: "For affectation appears, as you know, when the soul (*vis motrix*) locates itself at any point other than the center of gravity of the movement."[10] Rather than remaining the invisible motor of the body, affectation signals an incongruity or imbalance between center and periphery that produces an ungainly form that marks an absence (of grace) through a deviation or deformation of the body. Affectation is the result of being an object that is not one with its manner. The form of an appearance can be seemly or unseemly depending on the body's relation to signification, which marks the manner of its form and which in turn establishes the propriety or impropriety of its manner. It is not simply the body's relation to form but its form's signification that makes it mannered, ungainly, or awkward. The body's relation to signification makes it an object (that signifies) for another, determining it from an *ex-centric* point of view that displaces its center of gravity. The body's form becomes mannered, and it is affectation or manner that makes things both ridiculous and susceptible to ridicule.

As Kleist develops in "On the Marionette Theater," it is this reduction before the observant gaze of the narrator that turns a young boy into a ridiculous subject in his *earnest* attempt to repeat the pose of a sculpture. The young boy's slip from posture to imposture occurs almost imperceptibly before the gaze that establishes the nonidentity of his form with his manner.[15] Conversely, Kleist's strange description of the fencing bear's "utter seriousness" makes the bear completely immune to his human opponent's feints. At one with its manner, like a marionette, the bear's defense is impregnable. Lacking a relation to the form of its appearance, its manner, the bear cannot be tempted to fall for an appearance, a fencer's feint. Faced with this inhuman opponent, even a "gifted" fencer loses composure in his futile attempt to open up the space for ridicule. The ridiculousness of the bear's fencing mastery lies in its "utter seriousness." Only a subject incapable of objectification would itself be immune to deception and without a tell. Appearing without manner, such a subject would be truly inscrutable. Only a being in relation to its manner can fall for the mannerism of the other. If the most serious animals are also the most comic, as Baudelaire claims, citing the monkey and the parrot, it is because they seem to put on display their lack of relation to manner, rendering visible the very absence they are lacking. Lacking this lack they are at once ridiculous and beyond ridicule. It is this relation, i.e., being in relation to the manner in which this relation (this lack) appears to another that positions one in relation to the absent place of the signs that comprise one's manner. Unable to relate to the signs of their own absence, Baudelaire's comical animals may appear ridiculous but are not subject to ridicule. The capacity to relate not simply to oneself as an object but to its place, which is nonidentical with the object itself, makes one susceptible to ridicule, that is having one's manner mocked. Ridicule is thus the effort to put one in one's place.

The ridiculous tends toward ridicule when this lack serves to induce a belief in the norm (some propriety of manner) to which one is compelled conform, reinforced all the more as the subject ridiculed, i.e., the object identifies itself with *not* being an object. Only insofar as this *not* determines the object as object can the subject feel itself as an object. Ridicule aims to awaken the ridiculed to a flaw, a lack in/of its subjectivity, constituting a subject that is bound to the law's normativity through humiliation. The reduction of the ridiculed to nothingness positions it in the space of its own absence, and it is the exposure of an incommensurability between the object and its place that makes it funny. The ridiculous subject is thus not positioned as a subject but as an object out of place by the one who laughs at its lack, and it is this relation to the fact of its being an object in or out of place that makes this subject improper. The ridiculous subject is thus a ridiculous object that is compelled through ridicule to become a subject (a person like the one who ridicules) by identifying its own lack as improper. This negative attestation to propriety forces the ridiculed to identify not with the lack thus exposed, but with that to which the other's laughter attests. And this structural relation elevates the laugher over the laughed at. One escapes the humiliation of being an object (of ridicule) by escaping that which makes one laughable; one becomes a person by disidentifying, distancing oneself, from one's own impropriety. The one subject to ridicule thus identifies not simply with the one who laughs but with that which makes the laugher laugh, and it is this elemental splitting of the ridiculed object that makes possible its personification. The ridiculed subject, for ridicule to work, must aspire to being a person.

Ridicule aims to awaken the ridiculed to the intolerability of being an object, that is, a subject reduced to nothing. The division between being a subject and an object, and the maintenance of this division, lend much of the art of ridicule (i.e., caricature) a conservative function. This aims at conserving the norms that make a belief in *personhood* possible. Derisive laughter tries to restore the ridiculous subject to its place by ensuring the superiority of the one who laughs: "Look at me! I am not falling ... I am walking upright. I would never be so silly as to fail to see a gap in the pavement or a cobblestone blocking the way."[12] Derision thus aims at the restitution of seriousness, dreaming of a subject that is in control and that knows its place.

****

A pistol, so we are told, is the most severe of objects, a utensil to be handled with utmost care and, above all, *seriousness*. The pistol's sense, the seriousness of its tone, is bound up not simply with its function (the activation of its mechanism) but with the propriety of its use that assigns it a place and a value in the world. Like all products of work, it is justified by the gap it fills, the problem it presumes to solve. The pistol's mechanism, the engineering of its parts, is subordinated to a metaphysical end, its severity of purpose, whether employed for good or ill, that carves out for it a distinct value. An object whose aim is to make holes in things, its design presupposes the presence of a subject whose grip regulates and directs its use. The mechanical law governing its operation presumes a subject directing its aim, its objective, its target. The literality of its mechanism—the activation of the firing pin—presumes a metaphysical aim, a purpose: the maintenance and protection of the subject that controls its mechanism by being in relation to its end, its target. This subject is engendered by the belief in this aim. The pistol's sense is made possible by the difference and hence separation of the person responsible for maintaining its metaphysical rule from the mechanism itself, and this difference makes possible the subordination of the mechanism to its rule. The pistol's firing is occasioned by a person whose presence is assigned and made responsible by its directive. The sense of the pistol depends upon this harmonious synthesis of mechanism and purpose, defining the correctness of its use. The presence of Jarry, however, serves to upset this harmonious picture. Jarry's greatness lies in turning the mechanism of the pistol against its function, dislocating its metaphysical end. The pistol's violence is turned back against itself, against its sense, against the subordination of the mechanism to the proprietary rule of its handler. The pistol becomes a ridiculous sign, a symptom of insubordination.

As a ridiculous sign it signals a certain derangement, a sign of the absence of sense, of aim, of direction, where the mechanical function of this most dangerous of objects is unhinged from a directive or rule governing the propriety of its use. Rather than being informed through his relation to the pistol's end (its metaphysical objective), Jarry relates to its objectness (the sheer fact of its mechanism that goes off whether it fires or misfires). The function of the pistol is reduced to its dysfunction, the possibility of its misfiring. Without rule or governance, subject only to whim, the subject of Jarry is inscribed as a misfiring of the apparatus. The very fact that the object's mechanism could go off unintentionally shatters the illusion of safety dependent on the belief in the capacity of the person to make rational use of the mechanism, the belief that the law of its operation can be subordinated to a rule regulating its use.

The pistol acts; it goes off as if by accident whether the mechanism jams, fires, or misfires, whether it is loaded with blanks or bullets; and Jarry relates to the senseless effect of the mechanism's automatism. The pistol becomes the conduit through which an essential rupture is marked between Jarry, the person held responsible, and Jarry, the subject (of art). Jarry's identification with the pistol's lack of sense enables Jarry to divest himself from his belief in his person, making him a ridiculous *subject*, which is to say, an *artist*. Jarry is engendered by his belief in that which misfires rather than by the metaphysical belief in law and order. Jarry thus positions the artist beyond the *moral* purview of ridicule, in a manner that recalls one of Baudelaire's most *savagely comic* figures: the bad glazier.

****

In one of Baudelaire's most memorable outbursts of spleen, he describes a type of figure, "a certain nature" given to indolence and boredom, contemplation and reverie, who suddenly and impulsively acts with an impetuosity that surprises, first of all, the one who acts, overcome by a sudden need to shatter a convention, to test the limits of decorum, to upset an expectation, or to set in motion an ineluctable sequence that changes everything and cannot be reset. Such essentially destructive acts mark those moments in which the subject is acted, beset by an impulse, a sudden burst of energy that "hurls them into action by an irresistible force, like an arrow out of a bow."[13] Such subjects "discover in themselves at a given moment a lavish courage for performing the most absurd and the most dangerous acts," whose stupidity, whose sheer senselessness appears to turn them into victims of the whims of some malicious demon: the demon of the gratuitous, of *actes gratuits*.[14]

It is not I that acts, but it. Pinning itself to an act of caprice, such as the sudden seizure by an "arbitrary loathing" for a glazier, this subject commits its life to an erratic prank, a practical joke of "fortuitous inspiration" that risks eternal damnation for the "infinity of pleasure in a single second." When Baudelaire takes aim at the glazier's wares with a flowerpot from his sixth-floor apartment window, letting gravity do its work, who is the addressee of this declaration of war and its ridiculous command: "Make life beautiful!"? Of course, the explicit target is the glazier himself, who finds himself subjected to the poet's wrath for failing to have any colored glass: *a fault that is no fault of his own*. What the poet takes aim at in the glazier is precisely his moral fault that divides this subject through no fault of his own. But this failing is nothing more than the pretext for a burst of violence whose beauty consists in its arbitrary destruction. Make life beautiful! is a command that becomes a poetic assertion. It is an *act* of speech that turns language's declarative force into the programmatic equivalent of the poet's imagined violence. Poetry is beautiful when it awakens the object to its own division, a surface that registers the act that splits the poetic I. Poetry as a violent outburst of senseless energy, of spleen, that targets an object in order to display the effects of the "it" that acts, rendering manifest the gap in the I between the ego and *that* which acts. As an act, poetic assertion, like the self-destructive desire of the cigar smoker to light a cigar next to a powder keg, acts on the I, inflating it, intensifying it, by putting it at risk. The statement "Make life beautiful!" hurled at the glazier is in fact addressed to himself (the I) from a position eccentric to it (the satanic), for it is the arbitrary act itself that fulfills the requirement of making life beautiful. Only by being directed to an other does it hit the mark, namely the I divided by the act. The division of the I is monumentalized through an act that divides the other.

As Sartre suggests, Baudelaire's great effort lies in the strain to make that which acts (reflective consciousness) coincide with that upon which the act acts (reflected consciousness), as the blade in the act of cutting coincides with the wound.[15] Sartre writes, "If on the one hand he was the knife, the pure contemplative look which saw the hurrying waves of the reflected consciousness unfold beneath it, he was also and at the same time the wound, the actual consequence of those waves."[16] The dream of the purely arbitrary act, of *actes gratuits*, according to Sartre, seeks to break the circuit that sees the wound reflected in the steel of the blade, i.e., it dreams of an act that escapes the gaze that positions it, escaping from the paralysis of its own lucidity.[17]

> Baudelaire's fundamental attitude was that of a man bending over himself—bending over his own reflection like Narcissus. With Baudelaire there was no immediate consciousness which was not pierced by his steely gaze. For the rest of us it is enough to see the tree or the house; we forget ourselves, completely absorbed in the contemplation of them. Baudelaire was the man who never forgot himself. He watched himself see; he watched in order to see himself watch; it was his own consciousness of the tree and the house that he contemplated. He only saw things through this consciousness; they were paler, smaller and less touching as though seen though an eyeglass. They did not point to one another as a signpost points the way or a marker indicates the page, and Baudelaire's mind never became lost in their intricacies. On the contrary, their immediate function was to direct awareness back to the self. "What does it matter," he wrote, "what the reality outside me is made of provided that it helps me to feel that I am and what I am?"[18]

Yet Sartre supposes that *that which acts* is identical with consciousness. The fact that the self for Baudelaire comes into view through an act that deviates from an act of reflection can only indicate an essential imposture. The apperceptive moment in Baudelaire is occasioned by the arbitrary upheavals of the soul, the sudden impulses that misdirect it, violently altering its course, positioning him in relation to an object (the hurling of a word or a phrase) that upsets the tendential force of its reference, making Baudelaire, the poet, the instrument of the word, *not the director* of this destructive force. Yet, given Sartre's supposition, this can only be a simulation: "He simulated a disconcerting spontaneity, pretended to surrender to the most gratuitous impulses so that he could suddenly appear in his own eyes as an opaque, unpredictable object, appear in fact as though he were *Another Person*." For Sartre, Baudelaire thus fails to astonish himself, since it "would be an understatement to say that he divined his own plan before it was conceived." Sartre thus concludes: "Baudelaire was the man who chose to look upon himself as though he were another person; his life is simply the story of the failure of this attempt."[19]

Yet it seems to me that Sartre fails to adequately think what is at stake in this failure, which does not make Baudelaire a tragic but rather a comic figure. The figure of comic thought does not unfold within the element of reflection, but through repetition whose model is provided by the mime. "The pantomime," Baudelaire writes, "is the refinement, the quintessence of comedy; it is the pure comic element, purged and concentrated."[20]

****

Comedy, according to Baudelaire, falls into that "class of artistic phenomena which indicate the existence of a permanent dualism in the human being—that is, the power of being oneself and someone else at one and the same time."[21] Largely indebted to Rousseau's secularization of the theological model of the Fall, laughter for Baudelaire is an "expression, a symptom, a diagnostic"[22] of the soul's irreparable division, either observer or observed, subject or object, seer or seen. Comedy exposes and plays with the noncoincidence of a being whose sense of self is indexed to a fall, or better, a perpetual falling, whose disavowal suspends the laugher between two infinities. "Laughter is satanic," as Baudelaire writes, "that is to say that it is at once a token of an infinite grandeur and an infinite misery—the latter in relation to the absolute Being of whom man has an inkling, the former in relation to the beasts. It is from the perpetual collision of these two infinities that laughter is struck."[23] An integration that exposes a degradation, an identity that reveals a difference, laughter's convulsive character expresses "a double, or contradictory, feeling,"[24] as if revealing a being whose superiority lies in its capacity to render inferior. Laughter is fundamentally an expulsive movement, an outburst that acts as a disguise, marking a difference between being and its manner, by distinguishing the ridiculous manner of the other. Laughter is the assumption of a false identity, since it is predicated on a disavowal of weakness, of one's own susceptibility to disaster. When one laughs at the flaw in the object, it is not the object itself but its relation to the flaw that causes laughter. It is a cause that relates the lack in the object to the subject that avows it by disavowing its own: "The comic and the capacity for laughter are situated in the laugher and by no means in the object of his mirth."[25] Laughter becomes a form of blindness, which separates the form of the self/person from that which is lacking in it, constituting a sense of superiority—a difference in value between the superior and the inferior—that is illusory.

Yet, like the fetishist who, according to Freud, *disavows* castration—that lack in the mother of a phantasmatic object (the phallus)—laughter, according to Baudelaire, disavows the subject's division, maintaining a belief in its own superiority by differentiating itself from that which is lacking in the other, one's inferior. Paradoxically, laughter is a kind fetishism of the self. Ridicule and fetishism are inversely related. Whereas, according to Freud, the fetishist's identification with the object results in the splitting of the ego, in ridicule the laughing subject identifies itself through deriding the object. Both ridicule and fetishism involve a structure of disavowal (*Verleugnung*) that turns on a distinction between nothing and nothingness. If ridicule seeks to reduce something to nothing, the fetish elevates nothing to something. In both Marx and Freud, the structure of the fetish consists in attaching nothing to something (the negation of a social relation in Marx and the absence of the phallus in Freud), and that something (the commodity or the fetish) through this attachment, this relation to that which it is not, becomes something other. The object accrues an additional signification (an identity that includes its relation to what it lacks). The object becomes a sign that refers its identity to a negation. The fetish situates the fetishist in relation to a whole whose absence determines the sense of what is present. The fetishist is one who believes in nothing*ness*, and this belief attaches the nothing to a bit of material that serves as the *sign* of nothingness, marking a minimal difference between the nothing (the event of castration) and nothingness (its symbolic representation). To adopt Agamben's economic formulation: the fetish is "a negation and a sign of its absence."[26] The presence of the thing (the fetish) does not refer to the phallus, but to its lack.

It is this structural relation that characterizes disavowal. The fetish strangely refuses to consign the absence (of the mother's penis) to extinction by adopting surrogates that stand in for extinction, absence: not extinction of something, but the idea of extinction. The fetishist believes by making believe, discovering the unique power of the false. Freud writes:

> It is not true that, after the child has made his observation of the woman, he has preserved unaltered his belief that women have a phallus. He has retained that belief, but he has also given it up. ... Yes, in his mind the woman has got a penis, in spite of everything; but this penis is no longer the same as it was before. Something else has taken its place, has been appointed its substitute, as it were, and now inherits the interest which was formerly directed to its predecessor. But this interest suffers an extraordinary increase as well, because the horror of castration has set up a memorial to itself in the creation of this substitute.[27]

As a memorial to absence, the fetish is in relation to the absent (phallus) but not identifiable with it. It marks a minimal difference between the nothing and nothingness, negation and a sign of negation. The substitution indicates that something comes to occupy the very place of the absent, necessitating a distinction between the *structural* place of the absent and the *form* of that which occupies that place. Freud refers to the fetish as a compromise between the perception of a lack (castration), the anxiety it produces (the threat of loss), and the necessity of repressing (*verdrängen*) this anxiety. The fetish institutes a difference between affect and idea, such that the idea of absence remains but the affect (anxiety) attached to it is transformed; the fetish as idea alters the affect (anxiety) associated with the loss. It alters the affect by presenting the absence as attached to something (a foot, a shoe, or any object whatever). Disavowal concerns the displacement of an affect through a presence (the thing—any object whatever) that diverts or perverts the idea. The fetish positions the fetishist in relation to nothingness: a whole that appears through the part's relation to what it lacks. If the fetishist has always been inseparable from ridicule, it is because the peculiar identity of the fetish, like that of the ridiculed, is symptomatic of a subject that is not one with itself.

If derision aims to make the derided painfully aware of its deficiency, Baudelaire identifies what he calls the absolute comic, associated with the grotesque but above all with pantomime, with a lack of awareness: "one of the most distinctive marks of the absolute comic is that it remains unaware of itself."[28] Absolute comedy is not a matter of ridicule. It does not seek to reduce the one laughed at to nothingness, but produces a form of laughter that positions the subject in relation to the nothing (not nothing*ness*). This would be a form of laughter that situates the object and the subject of laughter in relation to the nothing, making laughter the expression of the not-wholeness of being. This is what I want to indicate with the ridiculous in contradistinction to ridicule.

The mime situates himself beyond ridicule since he does not pretend to be a subject but an object. Yet this lack has nothing to do with the "vegetable joy" of the innocence of a child's smile, which Baudelaire compares to a cat's purr or the wag of a dog's tail. "The comic can only be absolute in relation to fallen humanity."[29] The mime impersonates the parrot's seriousness, exposing the ridiculous by imitating the lack that removes the parrot from all subjectivity. The mime is the least tragic of figures, since he does not identify with his mask. He repeats, and it is this repetition that is ridiculous. Yet this repetition is not a repetition of anything other than the lack itself. That which is repeated is the nonreflexivity of division; the mime's lack of affection, its capacity to shield itself from humiliation (the affect of ridicule), derives from impersonation. It is not reflected in the other's gaze since the mime occupies the position of this other's lack. Occupying the place of this void, the mime repeats the place of the void. Baudelaire thus identifies the ridiculous as such with the grotesque. "There is but one criterion of the grotesque and that is laughter—immediate laughter."[30] The absolute appears comically through an "intuition" of a higher unity, and yet this unity is the unity of division. Baudelaire's own thought here reaches an impasse.

The absolute comic constitutes the artist as an exception to the "law of ignorance" that otherwise dictates the separation between the laugher and the laughed at. Internalizing this difference, the mime becomes the quintessential comic artist, a subject that makes himself ridiculous through becoming an absentee subject. Rather than the absolutizing of the subject, we find the absolutizing of the object qua subject. The ridiculous subject is positioned not simply as the object (as is the case in ridicule) but as a subject that performs, that is, repeats, its lack of awareness.

And it is perhaps for this reason that Baudelaire takes as paradigmatic the most savagely comic depictions of Pierrot.

> For some misdeed or other, Pierrot had in the end to be guillotined. Why the guillotine rather than the gallows, in the land of Albion? ... I do not know; presumably to lead up to what we were to see next. Anyway, there it was, the engine of death, there, set up on the French boards which were markedly surprised at this romantic novelty. After struggling and bellowing like an ox that scents the slaughter-house, at last Pierrot bowed to his fate. His head was severed from his neck—a great red and white head, which rolled noisily to rest in front of the prompter's box, showing the bleeding disk of the neck, the split vertebrae and all the details of a piece of butcher's meat just dressed for the counter. And then, all of a sudden, the decapitated trunk jumped to its feet, triumphantly "lifted" its own head as though it was a ham or a bottle of wine, and, with far more circumspection than the great St Denis, proceeded to stuff it into its pocket![31]

If the mime relates to the severed head as an indifferent object, as a ham or a bottle of wine, it is because the mime relates to the subject as nothing more than the division of an object: an utterly impersonal operation. The mime is the model of one who acts as an object, but not as a subject. The mime literalizes the expression "to think with your head." The sense of this formulation entails that one can think with one's foot, one's belly, or any other object, at the cost of stupidity. To think with any object other than the head is to misplace or displace the locus of thought. And in that case, if one loses one's head, the trunk had better bring it along. The mime relates to thought as a process of spatialization, as the distribution of places, of parts, and the mime often plays with that distribution, exhibiting the ways in which one can think with one's joints, the elbow, the knee, with one's manner. The mime is all manner, and it is this hollowing out of manner, the reduction of thought to the means of its manifestation, that makes the mime ridiculous.

****

To the question, Who are you? Jarry brandishes his pistol, the object that thinks in Jarry's place. This is doubtless a ridiculous answer, but an answer no more or less ridiculous than Diogenes' infamous and ancient attempt to introduce slapstick into philosophy. His most infamous of gestures, the presentation of a plucked chicken as a response to Plato's definition of man as a featherless biped, has little to nothing to do with a logic of refutation. It is not a matter of introducing a case that violates the rule, but of an act that puts the form of the question itself into question by taking aim not at this or that pretension to validity, but at validity as such. By comically conforming to the rule—by plucking the chicken—Diogenes suspends its constraining force. To the seriousness of Platonic inquiry, Diogenes proposes the ridiculous, the implosive power of non-sense.

Jarry thinks with his pistol, as Pierrot thinks with his head, Matisse thinks with his brush, or Freud thinks with his cigar.[32] The cigar becomes an *Arbeitsmittel*, as he puts it. Jarry's pistol is an *Arbeitsmittel*, or to adopt another of Freud's descriptions of his cigar, it is a weapon and protection against the lassitude, the pull of indistinction, indeterminacy, the vertigo of the abyss. It preserves distinction. The object becomes a non-sensical interval, a hyphen, that supports the passage of thought. As a hyphen, Jarry's pistol marks a disjunct in signification, a joint, a gash that opens up a gap, a hole, a crack, a seam. Now whereas we normally speak of a gash in the flesh, a gap, a hole, a crack in the surface, a seam between two pieces of fabric, the peculiarity of the hyphen as the event of he who pistols lies in its perversion of the logic of attribution. Jarry belongs to the event of the pistol as that which makes a hole in sense. To think *he who pistols* demands a perversion of sense in which one does not attribute the crack to the surface, the hole to the thing, but the surface to the crack, the thing to the hole; negativity is not in the thing (represented as an absence), but the thing is in it. The pistol absents Jarry as Jarry impersonates the pistol. Assuming Jarry's place, the pistol marks the void of his presence, making him ridiculous while protecting him from ridicule. The very sign of his present absence, Jarry's pistol serves to index an impossible subject as if impersonating a parrot's laughter.

This is the pistol's *patalogical* development, its unhinging of metaphysical attribution. The pistol marks an event, and Jarry is pinned as an effect of this encounter to this hyphen, this gap, that asserts itself as neither in the object (the pistol) nor in the person (Jarry). The pistol becomes a kind of mask, a mold of this crack, a capturing of its fault line, an impersonation of the void's surface, that refers Jarry to this act of the pistol's crack, making it impossible to discern whether the advent of he who pistols is a matter of filling a gap or punching a hole. As a pure mask, a pure persona (pure in the sense that it repels signification, signifying only its lack of signification), the pistol includes what it excludes (the relation to Jarry's person) and excludes what it includes (Jarry's personality); its outside is inside and its inside is outside. Put differently, as a pure hyphen—a dash, a strike—it renders indiscernible whether it is inside itself or outside itself.

The I of Jarry is pinned to a contingent preference, the pistol, whose nonsense positions it in relation to its own lack of significance, turning it into an autonomous fragment (differentiated from the whole), to which the *whole* of one's subjectivity is subordinated. In being attached to the object's negativity, whose act upsets the person of Jarry, the pistol marks the in-itself of that which is not itself. The identification of this event with the hole that the pistol makes in sense makes the I of Jarry *not whole*.

Jarry's relation to the pistol makes a hole in sense. The hole it makes paradoxically is not a hole in a surface; the pistol does not punch a hole within a whole that is constituted, but rather prevents the formation of the whole through the act of (hole) punching. The creative dimension of disavowal consists in the rigidification of the opposition that will provide a minimal structure that differentiates the pistol from sheer indeterminacy (its non-sense is always the non-sense of some sense), while preventing the institution of the whole. The structure is rather more like a weave, rattan, in which the holes are themselves composed through and by a structure of intersecting lines that form a surface with holes and gaps, rather than the holes being punched into a homogeneous surface. *He who pistols* is a weave, a structure whose composition is not in opposition to collapse.

He who pistols—this strange formula—rings out like a symptom. And the pistol is doubtless a fetish of sorts. However, if the fetish generally functions as an object that sustains the subject's belief in its own integrity, its identity *as a whole*, Jarry's pistol serves a counter function. The *pistol become verb*—this violation of the noun's grammatical identity—forces us to conceive *this object* as an event of an impersonal identity.[33] As an event of ossification, Jarry's fetish stages the I of this fetishist as dissolute: a subject declared by the object that speaks it to be *not whole*.

CHAPTER 5

COUNTING FOR NOTHING: THE NIHILIST

> At times, SOMEONE who is a complete stranger to the body and the sensibility speaks our words in *his own* interests.
>
> He sees and coldly describes life, death, danger, passion, everything in us that is human—but as someone else, a witness who is all mind. …
>
> Is it the soul?
>
> No. For this someone is, as it were, beyond all "affectivity." He is pure knowledge, with a peculiar detachment and disregard for the rest—like an eye that could see what it sees without giving any but chromatic value. … This *someone* would count the buttons on the hangman's coat.[1]

This one, this impersonal, radically detached operation of observation, stares with an alien eye and counts … coldly and lucidly bearing witness to its own nullity. This one would be like an eye that does nothing but mark the qualitative differences of a chromatic scale, inscribing differences as one cuts notches into tree bark. In counting, this one counts itself out, marking its absence, like an eye that sees without seeing an *object*, a being. Pure knowledge begins with the inscription of one's own absence like *counting the buttons on the hangman's coat*. Monsieur Teste—Paul Valéry's most strange, impersonal, and deeply nihilistic creation—is one who takes this SOMEONE into account. The pure witness of his own absence, he is a truly impossible subject. He is a nihilist, because he knows that he counts for nothing.

To count for nothing is the modern paraphrase of that ancient wisdom of Silenus that King Midas manages to finally goad from his captive: the terrible truth that it is better not to be born, and if born to die quickly.[2] If for the early Nietzsche this truth still elicits the heightened pathos of the "in vain,"[3] for Valéry's Monsieur Teste, this lucid witness (*testis*),[4] the excision of "man" from all meaning or aim is registered with the cool detachment of a counting machine. The subject of a pure formal operation, Teste, like the subject of science for Lacan, is "internally excluded from [his] object [*en exclusion interne à son objet*]."[5] only in this case, the object is himself. Teste says "I" as absent: a pure operation of excision where the person that thinks is attributed to the one (the alien within) whose count includes it as excluded. Teste is thought extracted from all affect, all feeling, all relation to sense (meaning and direction). As Jackson Mathews puts it, in his note to the English edition, "he is a mind behaving as a man."[6]

This makes Teste an utterly ridiculous subject: unfit to live, as Valéry suggests, even for an instant. To his infinite credit, however, this does not serve, for Valéry, to discredit Teste, to make him a laughingstock. There is plenty of humor in Teste, but not a hint of mockery. Teste is a figure of deadly seriousness because he exposes the true comedy of thinking. This unlivable observer, this fiction of thought, Teste—all head, all testicle—incarnates the instance of the subject as thought's ceaseless excision: "*the man of mind*," Valéry writes, "must finally reduce himself knowingly to an endless refusal *to be* anything whatever."[7]

Attesting to thought's relation to castration/decapitation (the excision of the *testis/tête*), Teste is an impersonation of the soul of thought as "the *hollow* form of a casket."[8] But how does one impersonate that which is not? A void? The nihilist: an I molded by nothing? Such questions become the concern of an art that takes counting in its most rudimentary form seriously. How to include the I as absent, to mark its void, its taste for decoys and surrogates? How to count for nothing?

A first step, perhaps, is the very leap Valéry takes in consigning himself to Teste's impossible logic, observing his machinations like an animal, to paraphrase Oswald Wiener, encountering a human being. Such detachment is indeed a beginning. Stripped of all pathos, becoming as ordinary as the nondescript objects populating Teste's abode, the horror of the void loses its menace. Assuming his existence as a matter of cosmic indifference, Teste submits to the rule of the one who counts. Counting the one in by making one count for nothing, Teste seeks thought's hollow form assuming itself with the vacant stare of one who confronts a stranger in the mirror.

****

As Kant observes, the difference between thinking and feeling marks the passage from the third to the first person. Kant writes,

> It is noteworthy that the child who can already speak fairly fluently nevertheless first begins to talk by means of "I" fairly late (perhaps a year later); in the meantime speaking of himself in the third person (Karl wants to eat, to walk, etc.). When he starts to speak by means of "I" a light seems to dawn on him, as it were, and from that day on he never again returns to his former way of speaking.—Before he merely *felt* himself; now he *thinks* himself [*Vorher fühlte es bloß sich selbst, jetzt denkt es sich selbst*].[9]

One feels an object, but one thinks a subject. One cannot feel an absence. The light that dawns on the child marks a shift in perspective in which Karl takes his absence for granted. The child enters into language fully only when it learns the "I" lesson (as Julien Torma puts it), when it learns that it, too, can count for nothing. Far from what language itself leads us to expect, the shift from the third person to the first is a movement of detachment, distantiation. The *emergence* of the first person is the least subjective of events. Thinking begins with this minimal separation from affection, which is first marked by the child's appropriation of the I to itself. The I takes possession of itself (the fact of its being an object) as an object. In representing itself as an object, it does not say I am something, but I am *not nothing*. Thinking begins when the I accompanies a representation (*Vorstellung*), indexing the difference between inscription (that which is felt) and registration (what can be thought). Thinking is made possible by this difference, when one does not simply take *oneself* into account (speaking in the third person), but takes *the* I into account, which is to say, the child forms a relation to its own absence: its lack of value.

Jacques Lacan at the beginning of the seminar on the four fundamental concepts of psychoanalysis introduces the problem of the signifier—the atom of all structural relation—at its most initial level as a matter of counting. In counting, the one who counts is already included in the count.

> It is only later that the subject has to recognize himself as such, recognize himself as counting [*comptant*]. Remember the naïve failure of the simpleton's delighted attempt to grasp the little fellow who declares—*I have three brothers, Paul, Ernest and me*. But it is quite natural—first the three brothers, Paul, Ernest and I are counted, and then there is I at the level at which I am to reflect the first I, that is to say, the I who counts.[10]

This bit of idiocy—this short circuit between the me and the I—reveals the failure of the simpleton or the young child to count the *exclusion*, i.e., the position of the I in the representation of the object. There are three brothers, but when I belong to the set, I must exclude myself (qua object) from the object of the count and include myself (qua subject). This shift from an external to an internal point of view transforms the form of the collection. The I belongs to it, but as an absent object. It is this capacity to position the place of its own absence, its signification, that enables the I to reflect the difference between being an identifiable object and being a subject that can think its position as an object. It is the marking of its *absence* that makes the I a matter of thought, as Kant puts it, and not feeling. When the I is *inscribed* in what it counts, its absence must be marked, that is, the I must *register* this inscription, which is to say, the *it* that inscribes. *Wo es war, soll ich werden*. The I (*ich*) appears in the absent place of the it (*es*) that counts. The idiot spontaneously *includes* himself in the count as an object (the *me*) and fails to take the place of the I into account, to grasp how it is included as absent. He says to himself: there are three brothers; the three of us are all brothers; I have three brothers. The ease with which one slips from the position of the object to the subject, from me to I, breaks down when one moves from the imaginary relation between the subject and the object to the symbolic relation. The idiot gives the lie to the belief that signifiers designate *something* and not *nothing*. To think is to think from the position of the idiot: to observe the shattering of an imaginary identity. The idiot makes the *me* suddenly appear as the obtrusive presence of an absence, like a hole filled in. The simpleton shows me that I count for nothing. If I am going to think, to escape idiocy, then I have to say, I thinks in me. I identify my image as an image of absence.

****

I need nothing. And even the word "need" has no meaning for me.[11]

Nietzsche defines the human as a "venerating animal,"[12] as an animal that *needs* to believe that it is *not nothing*, which places the one who *thinks*—who counts the I for nothing—into a strange dilemma. The one who thinks is not human.[13] As one who venerates, it believes, idealizes, and idolizes; and it is these ideals, these idols, these beliefs that imbue its life with meaning, with a sense of value, that give it direction and purpose, a place in the cosmic order. Such needs emerge as a function of its relation to lack.[14] It venerates only to the extent that it *needs* veneration. The destruction of an idol or an ideal points inevitably to the one who idolizes or idealizes, laying bare its excruciating *need* for the value that the idol or ideal bestows. Put differently, an animal that creates idols ascribes to the idol a power that it lacks, enabling it to believe that it is not nothing, that it is not for nought. The destruction of an idol, whether through a blow from a hammer (active nihilism) or through a deflationary wheeze (passive nihilism), results in the exposure of the nothing (the *nihil*) upon which the idol itself depends, bringing this creature who venerates face to face both with its utter insignificance and with its need, its pathetic need, to believe that it is worth something, that it, too, is venerable. "What we find here," Nietzsche writes, "is still the *hyperbolic naiveté* of man: positing himself as the meaning and measure of the value of things."[15]

The human venerates various things, various ideals, various gods, but in the last instance all veneration comes down to the need for meaning as such: that differential of value between something and nothing, being and not being, that lends the support of signification to its insignificant existence. The human being is something, i.e., something of value, only insofar as it is *not nothing*; and it is its relation to value that ensures this difference, which assigns it a meaning by assigning "the nothing that it is" the status of being "less than." It is this bestowal of meaning that differentiates it, ensuring that it is *not nothing*. It is value as such, signaled by a relation of dependency upon that which it is not, that differentiates the human (from mere nothingness) by assigning it a place that justifies its existence by distinguishing it from sheer indifference (nothingness). Belief in the venerable sustains the subject that venerates through the bestowal of a meaning upon its being: the difference between nothing and not nothing. It thus seems that to abolish one's venerations *tout court* (nihilism) entails the abolishing of the animal that believes (nihilism). Nothing prevents it from not being nothing.

The pathological form that nihilism takes—the pathos of the in-vain—depends upon the extent to which one still believes in the "purely fictitious world" that has been lost, for the universe itself can only be devalued if it had a value to begin with. The infamous wisdom of Silenus is addressed above all to this pathetic need. If the human being is better off dead, this is not because existence as such is without meaning, but is due to the human, all too human, need for it to be meaningful. Human woe is located in this metaphysico-religious—and sadly, as Freud puts it, all too infantile—need for wholeness (the oceanic feeling).

If nihilism understood as the devaluation of the highest values is symptomatic, as Nietzsche argues, of a will to nothingness that conceals itself in the maintenance of value (morality), meaning (metaphysics), law and order (the state), and causality (science)—all that gives *reality* a sense—the nihilist actively pits itself against these abstractions by isolating the symptomatic *need* to which they respond.

> *The perfect nihilist.* —The nihilist's eye idealizes in the direction of ugliness and is unfaithful to his memories: it allows them to drop, lose their leaves; it does not guard them against the corpselike pallor that weakness pours out over what is distant and gone. And what he does not do for himself, he also does not do for the whole past of mankind: he lets it drop.[16]

The nihilist actively forgets, cultivating an indifference to the "it was"—to those attachments that engender *resentiment*—by letting it go, while affirming decay by embracing the "corpselike pallor" of all ideals (the not-nothing). The *not*-nothing can either be more or less than nothing, and the nihilist lets it be less. He lets its need drop.

****

The nihilist separates itself from nihilism to the extent that one separates oneself from the pathological need for nothingness. It is this need, to be *not nothing*, that convinces the nihilist, according to Nietzsche, of *nothingness* as that truth that takes the form of a belief in negation (unbelief). Destruction becomes the means through which the nihilist separates itself from the not-nothing. To become enamored with the destructive act of negation itself, to identify with the lack in a given identification, is what Nietzsche calls "Petersburg-style nihilism (meaning *faith in unbelief* to the point of martyrdom)."[17] For Nietzsche the character Verkhovensky's infamous declaration "I am a nihilist, but I love beauty"[18] expresses the contradiction of the Russian nihilist as a figure whose belief in unbelief can only be sustained through an aestheticizing of destruction. Nihilism's will to truth compels the nihilist to sacrifice itself to nothingness in an effort to make the void appear as a vanishing conflagration, so as to produce, even if only for a fleeting second, nothingness, to see the nothing with one's own eyes, to bear witness, to attest, to prove the nothingness of all things. Kirilov's suicide is here exemplary. The nihilist believes all the more in its unbelief, making the sacrifice of belief into the ground of its belief in unbelief. In *Beyond Good and Evil*, Nietzsche poses the problem as follows:

> In rare and unusual cases, some sort of will to truth might actually be at issue, some wild and adventurous streak of courage, a metaphysician's ambition to hold on to a lost cause, that, in the end, will still prefer a handful of "certainty" to an entire wagonload of pretty possibilities. There might even be puritanical fanatics of conscience who would rather lie dying on an assured nothing than an uncertain something. But this is nihilism, and symptomatic of a desperate soul in a state of deadly exhaustion, however brave such virtuous posturing may appear.[19]

If this brand of nihilism is compelled by the need to *feel* nothingness, up to the point of its own contradiction, destruction, and martyrdom, it seeks to extinguish itself, to destroy all vestiges of its appearance as symptoms of insignificance. Such a project remains deeply *moralistic*. It retains a grip on the whole of value through its sequential destruction. Pathological nihilism exposes the extent to which the whole remains in play, as the image of Truth which knowledge of nothingness seeks to sustain. The Russian nihilist (as a type) practices the iconoclasm of an inverted religion, preserving a relation to the whole (nothingness) through the destruction of every last part. The perfect nihilist separates itself from this structural martyrdom by separating itself from all moral need (need for value).

Thus is born the image of the revolutionary nihilist: an idealizer in the direction of ugliness and a recurring figure within the avant-garde. Although no stranger to refinements of the *logos*, one of the most enduring features of this idealizer is a crudeness verging on asininity. The nihilist plays the dummy, the fool, the buffoon, a creature with a swollen big toe if necessary, assuming all that is repugnant in its combat against culture. Having stripped itself of the shield of Christian morality and its redemptive fable, the nihilist no longer believes that its suffering has a meaning. Fallen humanity is simply that.

Having lost all confidence that the lack of the good is anything other than its lack, the nihilist has nothing to separate it from its disgust. The human lacks, full stop. Identifying with the lowest, it takes aim at the highest. Abandoning propriety, decorum, and above all hygiene, the nihilist presents itself as the excrement erupting from Satan's anus, to borrow Martin Luther's diction. All the better to bring the ruckus, to stir up pandemonium.[20]

****

By counting the nothing in, the nihilist counts for nothing: the cost incurred, so to speak, for identifying thought itself with what Hegel terms the *monstrous power of negativity*. *Geist* as a devouring agent motivates itself by saying it is *not nothing*, attaching itself to that difference between nothing and nothingness by positing the former and negating the latter.

If the nihilist worries Hegel, it is because he has lost all faith in the other as the privileged site of recognition. Identifying itself, i.e., its *person*, with the mind's capacity to reduce all meaning and all value, all transcendence, to the *not* on which being as such surreptitiously depends, the nihilist identifies with the True as that moment of certainty in which the presumed or apparent consistency of some held belief, some *doxa*, which the subject holds to be true, unbinds the subject from all convictions that enable it to hold fast to reality.

If Kant only glimpsed this monstrosity at a safe distance, harnessing negativity to the task of transcendental synthesis, the nihilist locates the function of negativity not in the synthesis, in its relation of binding, in the capacity of the subject to formulate objectively correct propositions correlated to its phenomenal experience, but in its unbinding, dissolving, subtracting, and, in the last instance, destroying capacity.

Subject to a shattering event, that great unchaining of the earth from the sun,[21] the nihilist grasps that the world of meaning—to which we are condemned, into which we are thrown, to speak like a phenomenologist, and which affords us that battery of significations with which we outfit our burrow—undoes itself through its very articulacy. The nihilist sees its own blindness in the void's vacant stare. The significations that we have at hand cannot make sense of this event. The words we toss at this *thing* that happened are empty. Having become mere drool or babble, they lose their capacity to render distinct, to frame the catastrophe. They themselves become the bearer of a "malign opacity." They themselves become things: stuff taking up space. Sensitized to language's inbuilt betrayal, the word's blindness to its place, the nihilist cannot free itself from the sense that the very means through which the world opens itself to understanding comes at the cost of an opacity that situates the thinking subject in relation to an absence that decomposes, disintegrates, deinstalls the object of its concern.

The nihilist encounters at the heart of thought the sign's mute obstacle: the medium of all articulacy that bores into the real, marking the place of its absence like a fossil. The revelation of this void can be brute, cold, unrelenting, infinitely refined, crystalline and aridly lucid (consider M. Teste), but it can also follow a line of disorientation dictated by the passions (consider Artaud). Yet, however much it is filled with sound and fury, for the one touched by the materiality of its presence it signifies nothing.

As Hegel himself reminds us—even if he is often prone to forgetfulness on this note—Spirit's inseparability from the means of its articulacy entails that for all its forward progression, it constantly returns to the dead end that it drags along in its wake. It, too, gets lockjaw. Bone gets caught in Spirit's throat. The sign's mute materiality undoes the thought that thinks it just as it strips it of all affect. This is what Hegel intimates when speaking of bone: that impossible identification over which Spirit (*Geist*) stumbles, a dead end that presents consciousness with a nothing that cannot even be converted into the idea of its own nothingness, as if negativity itself was deprived of that "magical power" of converting the nothing into being. Spirit itself, of course, limps on, but the nihilist tarries with this destructive moment, feeling all too unconvinced by the transformative power of the negative, feeling it more honest to attempt to strip thought of its *Geist*, risking the scorn that the philosopher always reserves for the cynic and the stupidity of those who identify thought with the ultimate nullity of its substance: not death but bone. For Hegel, let us recall, identifying the life of the brain (consciousness) with the nullity that encases it (the skull or the *caput mortuum*)—passing off bone as the reality of consciousness—amounts to the "complete denial of reason."[22]

> The skull-bone is not an organ of activity, nor even a "speaking" movement. We neither commit theft, murder, etc. with the skull-bone, nor does it in the least betray such deeds by a change of countenance, so that the skull-bone would become a speaking gesture. Nor has this *immediate* being the value even of a *sign*. Look and gesture, tone of voice, even a pillar or post erected on a desert island, directly proclaim that they mean something else than what they *simply are* at first sight. They at once profess to be signs, since they have in them a peculiarity which points to something else, by the fact that it does not properly belong to them. A variety of ideas may well occur to us in connection with a skull, like those of Hamlet over Yorick's skull; but the skull-bone just by itself is such an indifferent, natural thing that nothing else is to be directly seen in it, or fancied about it, than simply the bone itself. It does indeed remind us of the brain and its specific nature, and of skulls of a different formation, but not of a conscious movement, since there is impressed on it neither a look nor a gesture, nor anything that proclaims itself to have come from a conscious action; for it is an actuality whose role it is to exhibit another sort of aspect of the individuality, one that would no longer be a self-reflected, but a purely *immediate* being.[23]

Sheer indeterminacy, utterly meaningless, the skull bone refers to nothing other than its own immediate, abstract, and empty being. Bone is that moment of absolute interruption—neither living nor dead—the advent of that which cannot die because life has no authority over it. Existence as such, without expression or indication, bone is but matter, less than nothing. The impossible incarnation of the void, only in relation to consciousness does it mark the place of an absence.

Like a sign reduced to its signifying material, it refers only to its own lack of reference, occasioning as if by chance sundry associations that nonetheless bear no resemblance to the indifference of its matter; a state of absolute repose, indifferent to all relation, it reflects nothing. And only in and through its resistance to all identification does bone mark that "intolerable state of suspended animation," that *repos*, Pascal writes, that "makes man experience 'his nothingness, his desolation, his inadequacy, his dependency, his powerlessness, his emptiness. Forthwith, there will rise up from the depths of his soul *ennui*, melancholy, vexation, despair.'"[24]

****

Bone marks the zero point of consciousness, its attachment to a mute obstacle, its absolute separation from itself. The nihilist, however, does not only attend to the manner in which consciousness is disrupted by its relation to its own natural being. It experiences this separation as a cultural phenomenon, as a disruption to the mechanisms of identification that inscribe the subject within the social field. Here it is not a question of the occlusion of consciousness (bone's nullity) but of a hyperconsciousness that disrupts itself. Such a subject experiences its culture as gangrenous, the installation of its values as something that rots away the interiority of its subjectivity, emptying its faith in language and the belief in its moral integrity.

The import of Diderot's *Rameau's Nephew* consists in describing this form of consciousness that "is a composite of nobility and baseness, good sense and irrationality."[25] In the "disrupted consciousness" of Rameau's nephew, Hegel discerns the movement of *pure culture* as the "absolute perversion" of consciousness into its opposite, the noble into the base, the high into the low. In Rameau's nephew the capacity to judge, to discern the good from the bad—the expression of a noble cast of mind—does not make him good or noble; the capacity to judge becomes the very means of separating noble consciousness from itself; that which serves to define it (its judgment) now serves to subvert it. Rather than defining noble consciousness, good judgment becomes destructive of it because its judgment is the very means through which it *appears* to be noble. It is its capacity for judgment that separates noble consciousness from itself. Nobility no longer appears to consciousness as a natural attribute but a *purely* cultural acquisition, a matter of pose and posture, something that can be bought and sold, exchanged. The subject that becomes truly conscious of this state of affairs (Rameau's nephew) inhabits society as a "nihilistic game," knowing full well that the capacity to judge the good and the bad has nothing to do with goodness or badness as such, just as what one says has little bearing on what one in truth means.[26] As is said of Rameau's nephew, "Nothing could be more unlike him than he himself is."[27] Rameau's nephew marks the destitution of the *honnête homme* and the pretensions of the *ancien régime* to legitimate itself through the aristocratic subject's capacity to model itself on classical philosophical virtue.

The subject of pure culture grasps itself as an empty form, nothing more than a social relation whose value lies in its social position. It grasps its own position as a disparity, an empty relation between two forms—nobility and baseness—whose content is a matter of posture, mannerism, and imitation. The subject's own integrity lies in accepting that it is a formal relation to an other that it internalizes.

The problem then is not that consciousness encounters an other that absolutely resists its identification (bone); rather its identity suddenly appears as something that consists in its dissolution. The romantic artist, in Hegel's analysis, is the figure who identifies the very substance of the subject with the process of its dissolution, with the satanic forces of disruption. The artist becomes the paragon of all creatures of culture, *a man without content*, to allude to Agamben's first book. Separated from its reality, the artist can only touch on the real through identifying with the disparity that marks this separation. Art likewise seeks its reality in itself—art for art's sake—locating its essence in the disparity of the real. Its central contradiction consists in attempting to make its form the very expression of its content: the work itself reduced to the subjective decision that gives it formal coherence, a movement of pure negativity, its content being nothing outside of the formal expression of its division. The romantic artist terminates in negation, suicide. Unsatisfied with negating the world, its quest for pure form can only turn on the subject whose content is its form: the romantic subject becomes the form of self-dissolution (*Selbstauflösung*): a self-annihilating nothing (*ein Nichtiges, ein sich Vernichtendes*). Agamben summarizes this situation well:

> Artistic subjectivity without content is now the pure force of negation that everywhere and at all times affirms only itself as absolute freedom that mirrors itself in pure self-consciousness. ... Inalienable and yet perpetually foreign to itself, art still wants and seeks its law, but because its link with the real world has grown weak, everywhere and on every occasion it wants the real precisely as Nothingness: art is the annihilating entity that traverses all its contents without ever being able to attain a positive work, because it cannot identify with any content. And since art has become the pure potentiality of negation, nihilism reigns in its essence.[28]

Art then, like the bone, is an annihilating entity not because it reduces everything to death, but precisely because it is unable to die, separating itself, in its nullity, from any sense-giving negativity. *Art as the mummification of spirit.*

****

The nihilist's violence is directed at reality as such. That is, the nihilist violates the words and images that frame reality's manifestation, challenging the self-evidence of the syntheses that make its cognition possible. Once manifestation as such, the *aesthetic*, becomes suspicious, once the seen and the said betray a duplicity of intent, the signifying structure of reality assumes the character of a conspiracy and thought itself begins to *revolve* "*around delirium as its axis*."[29] Delirium becomes the medium, the atmosphere, of nihilist thought, which divides itself between the extremities of science and art, nature and culture, truth and fiction.[30]

In the name of science, as that thinking that installs the nothing as its formal pivot, the nihilist apprehends the subject as counting for nothing. It counts for nothing both in the idiomatic sense of being without value and in the literal sense of being counted in as out, included as an absence (what Jacques-Alain Miller referred to as the suture of the subject).[31] Science presents the nihilist with the truth of subjectivity as the marking of its void, the prefiguration and presentiment of its absence. The nihilist subject sees itself in the hole that science makes of it, engendering an imaginary that has yet to be outstripped by Edgar Allan Poe's "William Wilson" where the narrator, finding himself in that most uncanny of traps, becomes the narrator of his own absence by becoming the murderer of himself: "You have conquered, and I yield. Yet, henceforward art thou also dead—dead to the World, to Heaven and to Hope! In me didst thou exist—and, in my death, see by this image, which is thine own, how utterly thou hast murdered thyself."[32] If science marks the subject as a lack in its signifying structure, art presents the subject of the artist as an empty person, a mask, a persona.

****

Such a subject no longer experiences itself as a *person* endowed with inalienable qualities, but as a set of reflective operations (M. Teste), as a marionette deprived of grace (Kleist), as a tailor's dummy (Bruno Schulz), as a machine (Andy Warhol); at its most extreme, the nihilist experiences itself as "a vacancy absorbing space" (Helen Keller and Roger Caillois). Everything that is one's own, that one would associate with one's innermost property, suddenly seems to be the possession of something else, an alien being, that has awkwardly assumed one's place. One experiences oneself as a *persona*, a being acted by another, a mask covering the face of the void, a thing impersonated by another. "The stranger's way of looking at things," Valéry writes, "the look of a man who *does not recognize*, who is not of this world, the eye that is a frontier between being and not-being—belongs to the *thinker*. It is also the look of a dying man, of a man losing *recognition*."[33] Teste is his own double, the strange look at things translated to the appearance of a man so ordinary that his person loses all discernible quality, becoming a mere thinking *thing*. Teste is an impersonation of thought: the personality of a thought that no longer recognizes its relation to the person. "The mind must not be concerned with persons. *De personis non curandum*."[34] In the Christian tradition, the human *person* came to connote the spiritual core of the individual, the soul's imprint; with Teste, it is restored to its etymological roots in the Greek, *prosopon* (mask), as the very face of the void.

Up steps the dandy: the figure who knows that the soul in-exists, but performs it nonetheless, attaching its thought to the ephemera that compose the skeletal architecture upon which the soul is then hung. If there is a camaraderie between the dandy and the nihilist, it consists in their shared grasp of the liquidation of meaning and perception, that value has to be made to undermine value: turned outside in and inside out. One undermines the belief in the nothingness, the value of value, by disbelieving in the person, making the subject the site of its interruption, making use of the nothing to undermine nothingness.

The dandy grasps what Nietzsche refers to as the inconsistency of the nihilist's pathos: "A nihilist is a man who judges of the world as it is that it ought not to be, and of the world as it ought to be that it does not exist. According to this view, our existence (action, suffering, willing, feeling) has no meaning: the pathos of 'in vain' is the nihilists' pathos—at the same time, as pathos, an inconsistency on the part of the nihilists."[35] *Counting for nothing*: the nihilist is divided along the lines of the ambiguity of this English idiom which marks in one stroke the void of value and the value of the void. An irreparable tension that Teste registers laconically on his deathbed: "After a while, before the finish, perhaps, I shall have that important moment—perhaps I shall behold the entire sum of myself in one terrible flash. ... Not possible."[36]

****

Before his death, Valéry was preparing material to be added to a new edition of *Monsieur Teste*. The English edition fittingly ends with Teste ruminating on death. "It is a matter of going from zero to zero. And that is life. From the unconscious and senseless to the unconscious and senseless."[37] If the nihilist's adage of despair runs something like: "Everything comes to not and not comes to everything," Teste subtracts all pathos from this adage, making it the expression of a logical identity. As the subject of thought, Teste is included as object as an absent subject. Thinking is a matter of going from zero to zero.

o = o. In thought, the subject implicated in its count is identified with the moment of separation that makes possible a fatal conclusion that Jean Amery calls the logic of death:

> The *logic of death* is not a logic in the usual sense, upholding reason alone, for it allows no conclusion other than just one, again and again and again: not is the same as not, with which the statement of every logical (that is, analytic) judgment, already in itself containing no reality, loses its last tie to reality; that tie above all in which the equation of two categories of being that are symbolically recorded as in mathematics, or are rooted in everyday language, is now related to something that is nothing and is not—a pure negation, an accursed inconceivability.[38]

This logic paradoxically sets out of joint the very hinge upon which logic turns: the principle of identity. The logic of death binds a category of being, namely nonbeing, to the symbolic mark of negation, the void (o). The logical identity thus includes its own nonrelation to reality. Logical identity—the very essence of thought—becomes the direct expression of an *accursed inconceivability*. In death, reality touches upon its real through its abolition. The absolute real, that tie which unbinds, has the least reality. Not = not finds no basis in reality, in the conditions of possible experience. The realization of logic, the logical act, as the identification of the void is set against the synthesis that makes a given reality possible.

The figure of Teste, the impersonation of thought, poses the problem of a life thought as the progress—instantaneous and lumbering—of o to o. "'Well' (says M. Teste). 'The essential is against life.'"[39] What *sense* can this passage from o to o have, especially considering that this passage itself constitutes Teste's impossible identity? Teste grasps that he (as thought) has no existence outside the very materiality of these markers of absence. He apprehends that he (as subject) is inscribed within them inexorably and without affectivity. The passage of thought can include itself in what is here given to thought only through the division that these material marks themselves institute: a division that registers the differentiated place of their space. Mute and senseless inhabitants of place, they make thought possible. The exigency of thought's attachment to senseless material serves to separate the thinking subject from the unthought, which is the skeletal structure of every thinking. Bound to the senseless markings of his proper name, Teste's I is situated by the letters that pry open a gap between matter and its place, and that present him absently. "I am the unstable," Teste states: an I that that identifies a point of "maximum incoherence."[40]

Thought, like its name, Teste, bears witness to a most ancient thesis: that of atomism. Althusser ingeniously condensed the radicalism of this thought into the formula: the *nonanteriority of meaning*. Thinking happens, it is a senseless event—the only *thing* that matters to Teste—and it happens as the irreducibly contingent splitting into *atoma* and *kenon*, atoms and void.

Thinking imbues thought with the void, marking the gap between thinking and thought as the gap between atom and void, turning its support into a living corpse.[41] Thought has a morbid elegance. As Jacques Rigaut utters beautifully: "Essayez, si vous le pouvez, d'arrêter un homme qui voyage avec son suicide à la boutonnière." (Try, if you can, to stop a man who travels with his suicide as a boutonniere.) Teste, nihilist and dandy, is the living *incarnation* of lack, a suicide *avant la lettre*, a figure with a black carnation in his lapel.

CHAPTER 6

SLIPPERED NEGLIGENCE: THE DANDY

> The meaning-factory that I (joylessly) am is hermetically sealed off, and so I am free—as soon as I can shed my conditioned fear of the consistency business—to attack any meaning that threatens to take control of me. To make cynical use of the language of the prisoners of language: the light only goes out when the skull slaps against the wall. But sleight-of-hand, however radical, still has its laws. The world of "anything goes" is pink noise, and as such is dependent on a recording apparatus. That is to say, random space has structure.[1]

Like the nihilist, the dandy is a figure on the brink of vacancy. Dealt in as a dummy hand, this figure relates to its being as a bluff, a gambler indifferent to loss. If vacancy is presumed, value liquidated, the fundamental problem remains that of the *brink*. This is where the dandy wagers its being.[2] Embracing the throw of the dice, the accidental and the contingent, the fortuitous detail, mere filigree, some signifier occasioned by chance that makes the difference, the dandy lends the void a luxurious air, a crystalline refinement, an elegant ease, or, as William Hazlitt beautifully writes, "a slippered negligence."[3]

If dandyism, as Baudelaire writes, "is the last spark of heroism amid decadence"[4]—and Joris-Karl Huysmans's depiction of Jean des Esseintes in *À Rebours* (*Against the Grain*) takes this heroism to a truly ridiculous and decadent extreme[5]—the dandy marks the triumph of hyperbole. Polishing one's boots with nothing but the froth of champagne, lighting up a banknote to help a rich financier look for some small change lost in the dark, dreaming like Fitzcaraldo of an opera house in the jungle, or having a favorite foot, the dandy treads the thinnest of lines between sense and nonsense.

Speaking of Beau Brummel as an ephemeral creature of gesture and a minimalist of wit, William Hazlitt writes:

All his *bon-mots* turn upon a single circumstance, the exaggerating of the merest trifles into matters of importance, or treating everything else with the utmost *nonchalance* and indifference, as if whatever pretended to pass beyond those limits was a *bore*, and disturbed the serene air of life. We have heard of

"A sound so fine.

That nothing lived 'twixt it and silence'"

So we may say of Mr Brummell's jests, that they are of a meaning so attenuated that "nothing lives 'twixt them and nonsense'": —they hover on the very brink of vacancy and are in their shadowy composition next of kin to nonentities. It is impossible for anyone to go beyond him without falling flat into insignificance and insipidity: he has touched the *ne plus ultra* that divides the dandy from the dunce. But what a fine eye to discriminate: what a sure hand to hit this last and thinnest of all intellectual partitions![6]

Like the fetishist, condemned by the man of Enlightenment for caprice and whimsy, the dandy pins its subjectivity to a trifle. Relating to its manner of appearance and speech as both the only confirmation of its being and its consummate betrayal, the dandy attaches its identity to the disjunction (the brink) where that which lacks sense assumes the sense of its lack.

Not an entity but not a nonentity, the dandy's subject comes undone from the particles that place it. If the dandy believes with Freud that style makes up the human (*Le style, c'est l'histoire de l'homme*), it is because the human is always on the verge of being nothing more than a mere heap of clothes.[7] Placed then at the bind/unbind at which the subject appears as a thing identifiable, that is, as a person, the dandy is a detached observer of its self, its situation, and the social relations on which it depends. The dandy is inside out, an outsider on the inside, and it is in this sense that the dandy aspires "to be sublime without interruption; he must live and sleep in front of the mirror."[8]

If the figure of Monsieur Teste is the *end* of dandyism, in the sense of being its most extreme possibility, as Oswald Wiener claims, it is because, identifying with nothing, counting for nothing, he comes to observe the void of his constitution. Teste grasps the subject as a game played between the I and the me, which is to say, a game played between oneself and the void of one's constitution (a relation to the other). The other, like oneself, for Teste, i.e., for the dandy, cannot be posited as a *person*, for like oneself it must be grasped as a thing acted by another.

The game played with oneself.

The effect on others must never forget mechanics—quantities, intensities, potentials—and treat them not only as themselves, but as machines, and animals—whence an art.[9]

The strained lucidity of Teste's self-relation makes his relation to others equally strained and awkward. His speech is not addressed to the other person, but to the Other in the other. Addressing his speech to *nobody*, each of his utterances drops like a stone: "To what he said, there was nothing to reply. He killed polite assent. Conversation was kept going in leaps that were no surprise to him."[10]

Figures that make speech uneasy, whether in the manner of Teste or of Brummel, prove always in the end to be unwanted guests. Provocations that make us aware of our perilous proximity to the void awaken in us an anxiety that the structures upon which we depend for our very existence—signifying and social—are nothing stable. Such provocations are of course a nuisance and must be liquidated, got rid of one way or another. "The anxiety of dandyism," Wiener writes, is provoked by "the threat of the cataclysm [more literally, flood] of the unconscious [*bedrohung durch die flut der unbewussten*]."[11] Figures like Beau Brummel or the Marquise de Merteuil had to be disappeared, exiled to the social margins, according to Wiener, since they exposed "a hidden mechanism"[12] that gives the lie to self-possession and, for that matter, all other naturalizing mechanisms that attempt to explain the fate of the human being—its identity, its social place, and self-worth—as anything other than aleatory. A figure at home in the uncanny (*das Unheimlich*), the dandy's ease with its *thingly* character and loss of identity helps to equip those of us concerned with the prospect of being buried alive.

****

In the essay "Eine Art Einzige" (A manner singular), Oswald Wiener takes his point of departure from Baudelaire's interest in the dandy, framing his discussion through reference to Valéry's *Monsieur Teste*. The dandy form, for Wiener, essentially unfolds between Baudelaire and Teste. What interests Wiener is "a singular characteristic [*ein einziger zug*]" of the dandy: "dandies are still metaphysicians."[13] This is not to say that the dandy is a philosopher or that he produces an articulated system. The dandy is certainly not without theoretical interests, or an interest in theory, but, as Wiener stresses, it is only ad hoc, proceeding by means of "maxims, propositions, aphorisms."[14] The dandy's practice, however, does produce a spontaneous metaphysics that Wiener attempts to extract by attending to the dandy's distinctive *phronesis* (practical intelligence).

What distinguishes the dandy has nothing to do with the sartorial, or at least this is a secondary phenomenon, "the vulgar phase of dandyism."[15] The focus on appearance for which the dandy has become an identifiable type (such calculability being precisely anathema to the dandy) misleads, or better, distracts from the true focus: the concern with the subject's absence. The dandy is constituted as an observer of its own disappearance. A singular witness to what Verena von der Heyden-Rynsch (a feminine heteronym of Oswald Wiener), in the afterword to the collection *Riten der Selbstauflösung* (Rituals of self-dissolution), calls "the automatizing of groundlessness. Meaning slips away, the grid remains."[16] The dandy's art concerns the place of the subject in the grid, the role it plays within a given structure. The dandy's practice embeds an experimental form of cognition in which an engagement with the other (conceived broadly: other persons, society, language, etc.) occasions a complex play in which the place of its own subject is marked as absent (within/from the structure). By marking this place, the dandy separates itself from all content, i.e., from the belief in the person.[17]

The dandy constantly tests the sense in which it can be *said* to be human, conscious, intentional, etc. without presuming such determinations to be the case. Assuming the self to be artificial (*kunstlich*)—the self (person) as a matter of production[18]—the dandy investigates, through the reactions it provokes in its social context and in itself, the extent to which it is a *thing* (in the sense explored by John Carpenter's *The Thing*: a being that has no content outside of its resemblance). Rather than opposing the self to "ordering mechanisms" (the rules) that structure its relation to its environment and to itself, the dandy assumes its subtraction from meaning and intention in an effort to break with the naivety of its own action: "from self-observation we know that our activity almost always short-circuits; that is, our models obviously touch upon only its surface without its relations to patterning, validity, or modification being subject to test. in this narrow sense, the *artificial* exists only in the vicinity of the creative moment, it *is* the creative."[19] The dandy is an artist only to the extent that it is artificial, i.e., its relations (self and social) are determinable through the structural mechanisms that lend formal determinacy to any given content. The outside of any given structure can only be sought within a given structure.

Opposed as much to Rousseau's and Schiller's conceptions of the natural as to the Marquis de Sade's Satanic conception, the dandy identifies with the moments of short circuit within the structure of its behavior, the deviations, in other words, of the law from itself. Abandoning as wantonly utopian the belief in the feasibility of transgression, the dandy is closer to Melville's Bartleby or Beckett's figures of exhaustion. The dandy's opposition to society, like its opposition to law, derives from an opposition to what such laws render possible *and* impossible, namely a belief (essentially utopian) in that which is outside of the law: nature. Torma is dandyesque when he writes: "The vanity and ridiculous pretentiousness of *ornament* (style, decoration, architecture ...) confer upon it all its value. I care about ornament because everybody likes it, and that's the way to pay THEM back in their own coin."[20]

****

The dandy's protest, for Wiener, is "not directed against a certain state or any other folklore, but against the state, language, consensus, processes, models, 'rules governing thought,' not against behavioral styles but against the forms of one's way of thinking."[21] This is the way in which Wiener's, but also Konrad Bayer's, interest in the dandy converges with the concerns animating their own artistic experiments and that of the Vienna Group. The singularity of the dandy lies in having at once abolished the notion of interiority (an inner self that would disclose itself through reflection) without ceding the position of the subject to mechanical explanation (which would amount to nihilism: "of course the rejection of the subjective meaning is precisely what constitutes the nihilist").[22] There is a singularity of the subject, but it is not to be found in the so-called *personal* (the content of the individual). Subjective distinction, in contrast to personal eccentricity, can only be located in the practice of experimentation itself: in the dandy's practice of gleaning reactions provoked in a given social situation. The dandy's practice aims to counteract its effect, deviating, however slightly, from the laws that structure any given situation: to act and not just react.

The dandy observes its person in the effects it produces in the other and locates its subjectivity in the act that *disidentifies* with that person (i.e., the person it has become). Having divorced the problem of the self from romanticism's concern with interior depth, the dandy accepts the artifice of the emotions—the life of the passions, too, follow automatic laws. The dandy thus does not differentiate the "interior life of the passions" from events unfolding within the world; this privilege of the person and impulsive reaction must be neutralized. As Baudelaire writes, "A dandy may be blasé, he may even suffer; but in this case, he will smile like the Spartan boy under the fox's tooth."[23] Like a good Kantian, the dandy treats inner and outer sense (intuition in Kant's sense) as equally phenomenal, that is, as conditioned by the a priori of time and space whose *objective* determinations gain meaning or significance (Sinn) through the transcendental laws that synthesize intuitions and concepts. This procedure removes the question of personal identity (the problem of consciousness as posed by Locke) from subjectivity proper. The subject of experience is not given in experience, but deduced as the empty operation that makes identification itself possible: *a spiritual automaton* in the most radical sense.[24] The singularity of the subject (which by force of habit we assign to interiority), for the dandy, is made to surface from the position of the observer (the outside). The dandy occurs as an inward torsion of the social space it inhabits: as Wiener puts it, "the dandy is located as an inward spiral."[25]

This is not to say that the dandy is a mere reflection of its environment. Baudelaire's famous proposition that the dandy "must live and sleep in front of a mirror" does not turn the dandy into Narcissus. Far from being absorbed in self-contemplation, the dandy in the mirror of society faces an other (like itself and yet hostile, as Lacan discerns) from whom it must infer its own identity. If the "normal" subject interiorizes this identification, the dandy's rigorous and artificial procedure reverses this normal process: externalizing, disidentifying with its *semblant*, i.e., with the person it appears to be. As Teste the consummate dandy declares: "Imagine thinking our own image is not indifferent to us!"[26] The dandy attributes to the other everything that one would normally claim for and as oneself. One's image is but the image of the other and thus, if not indifferent, must be made to be so. The dandy thus appears to itself as other, literally incarnating that most uncanny of Rimbaud's poetic propositions: "I is an other [*je est un autre*]."[27]

To speak of alienation here is much too weak, since the dandy undoes the presumption that posits recognition as a need. The despair of the dandy, its subtraction from hope, concerns the dandy's assumption of the structural function of its own absence. Wiener writes,

> yet he gives up everything that he understands about himself, none of which he can love as a component of his own personality; he yields that which has been understood about himself over to that which has been understood about the other. the other indemnifies him through his exposure of the mechanical meaninglessness of his life's course; he is the bearer of all the hopelessness that has been perceived in his own life ... it is not important that he love himself—not many dandies do—but that he protect something that would give love meaning ... "in front of the mirror" means here: to observe what cannot be perceived differently, to know which impression the strange outside will make on the strange eye, to study in oneself the automatism of the strange eye, and to cultivate what withdraws from all of this. also, the emptying of the world is neither paranoid nor schizophrenic; it follows from the study of societal forms.[28]

The other exposes the dandy to its structural meaninglessness, allowing it to see its absence in the strange eye that configures its image from which it disconnects. The dandy thus lucidly assumes itself as the bearer of the hopelessness of which its image has become a sign.

****

For Oswald Wiener dandyism is the paradoxical art that attempts to make a form of that which escapes the law of formalization. Recognizing its relation to the other as its only content, the dandy seeks to constitute itself through a constant disidentification with the form of its appearance, which the dandy gleans through the other's provocation. This art lies in treading the thin line between distinction and indistinction, so that the dandy can singularize the absenting of the subject, marking the wisp of a difference (the infrathin) between character and characterlessness, charm and insult, value and valuelessness, wit and stupidity, being a mere object and an intentional subject. The dandy actively identifies with the slight deviation, the swerve (the *clinamen*), the contingent impression, the singularizing detail, or the slightest inflection of the sign: anything to make sense tend toward non-sense. To speak a language *like* a human, i.e., as a subject, imitating a parrot; to mark the difference within the automaton itself of that slight glitch that makes a subject—that is, an *it that thinks*: this is the object of the dandy's practice, as if attempting to observe the emergence of that difference that frames the place of the subject in the machination of an automaton. Valéry's *Monsieur Teste* pushes this attempt, according to Wiener, to its limit: "Valéry tries to present Monsieur *Teste* as a human would appear to an animal."[29]

Far from simplifying Baudelaire's identification of the dandy, as is the case, according to Wiener, with Huysmans's "vulgar equation" in *À Rebours* of the dandy's decadence with illness,[30] with M. Teste sickness itself becomes a form of cognition.[31] The very notion of self-identity, of character itself, has dissolved and been replaced with the problem of self-observation. As the narrator in an "Evening with M. Teste" asks, "What had he done with his personality? How did he regard himself?"[32] It has disappeared into the name. Edmond Teste serves merely the *nominal* function of naming a set of abstract operations. Wiener writes, "he no longer concerns himself with his self [*mit sich selbst*], but with the form in which he appears to himself in his ideas; his identity is provisional."[33]

With Teste, *everything* is external—words like things and things like words—serving only to mark the distance between a projected interiority and its surface, incisions into space that build a hollow whose repetition provides the outline of a thing in variation, plastic, malleable, infinitely receding: "the *object*, the terrible *object*" of "inner sight."[34] This *object* is what is at stake in all of Teste's speech, his perambulations, and even his sleep. It is that thing which he is, but from which he is removed: "He spoke, and one felt oneself confounded with *things* in his mind: one felt withdrawn, mingled with houses, with the grandeurs of space, with the shuffled colors of the street, with street corners."[35] Teste relates to himself as a word become thing, as if he is speaking bits of matter. *Thingly* words lose their sense, and Teste uses words to confound not simply word and thing, sense and non-sense, but even the *expectation that one is speaking after all with a person*.[36] Teste can indeed be eloquent, we are told, making fine use of "touching words—the very ones that bring the author closer to us than any other man, those that make us believe the eternal wall between minds is falling,"[37] but he adds to them an inflection or subtracts a sentiment that removes them from sense:

> The ones he used were sometimes so curiously held by his voice or lighted by his phrase that their weight was altered, their value new. Sometimes they would lose all sense, they seemed to serve only to fill an empty place for which the proper term was still in doubt or not provided by the language. I have heard him designate a simple object by a group of abstract words and proper names.[38]

The strangeness of Teste's speech consists in his extreme nominalism. He sheds any residual belief in language's transparency. Words refer and identify at the cost of an irrevocable and necessary betrayal that makes the illusion of communication possible. The subject's dependence on language, for Teste, makes articulation a ceaseless externalization of that which is interior, making even the most intimate of internal monologues a process of hollowing out.

Rather than positing Teste within a field of meaning, his relation to linguistic structure serves to separate him from meaning. He acknowledges him*self* as an effect of this structure. With Teste the problem of the dandy touches upon that of the nihilist. Teste is excruciatingly aware of the separation of the subject's identity from meaning: that who he is "cannot be differentiated from the position of the other and that each of his insights occur to him [i.e., the other in him] and that he is only incidentally and insignificantly the one to whom they happen."[39] *He-who-observes* is who he is, and this insight can only lead to "the impossibility of identifying with the *content*" of any given act of observation. He *is structured*. Teste's existence cannot be distinguished from the position of the other whose position in him serves in turn to divide him from all content: "the observing instance in him becomes strange to him."[40] Separated from himself, he becomes the indirect object of his own act that prompts him to identify with the act that divides his identity. The other in him is what speaks.

Teste relates to his character (personality) in the same way that he inhabits space, "like geometry's *any point*."[41] Identifying his voice as the anonymous voice of the other that speaks in him, Teste becomes a neutral *it* that speaks, that marks and observes from a space defined as nondescript. As the narrator describes Teste's lodgings: "My host existed in the most general interior" sparsely populated with "dull abstract furniture—the bed, the clock, the wardrobe with a mirror, two armchairs—like rational beings."[42] Radically impersonal, the ordinariness of Teste's external space, which the narrator observes with "horror," reflects the "extraordinariness" of Teste's mind: "'You know a man who knows that he does not know what he is saying!'"[43] Socratic wisdom—knowing that one does not know—with Teste is oddly reversed, because he knows that he does not know *what he is saying*. Teste knows that he is spoken by language, making all knowledge of the self a knowledge of an irrevocable externality, since one is not identical with what one says.

****

Teste inhabits his relation to himself as a labyrinth whose structure is itself devouring. It is not the Minotaur at the heart of the labyrinth that is of concern, since there is no center and hence no threatening beast that awaits. More daunting is that the structure itself has become monstrous: the horror horribly banal and all the more horrible since there is no escape.

Or perhaps the more appropriate metaphor is that of a crime scene. If "one should go into himself armed to the teeth,"[44] as Teste writes in his Logbook, it is because one is entering a space that is structured like a mystery, "a tale of ratiocination." Like the Chevalier C. Auguste Dupont, Teste proceeds by "ratiocination" alone—entering interiority like an exterior space riddled with the signs, the remains, to be more macabre, of his own absence. To speak is to be caught up in an intrigue, and Teste is a subject that knows that he is ensnared by structures on which he nonetheless depends. The subject is only a subject as caught up in an intrigue, a conspiracy, and the ultimate conspiracy always amounts in the end to the subject's own abduction, its death and/or disappearance.

Wiener alludes to the dimension of intrigue in Edgar Allan Poe's "The Murders in the Rue Morgue," and he views a character like Dupin as "at once a deepening and flattening of the possibility" of the concept of intrigue developed by Choderlos de Laclos with the figure of the Marquise de Merteuil.[45] However, such flattening is the dandy's prerogative, and it is always the measure of elegant poise to see how such figures can maintain the slight cock of the chin while encountering some black ice. Will they crack up, like Jerry Lewis who slips from every surface in a Lucite world?[46] Or will they become a piece of "incomprehensible still-life"?[47] Both are certainly strategies, no doubt, for turning the ridiculous to one's advantage.

Both the Marquise's and the Chevalier's sculptural poise—that is, Dupin's—stems from their lucidity: to believe in interiority as some hidden lock box is for them both an abominable illusion. Neither of them makes much ado about this "discovery." They possess it as a banal rather than a disturbing truth. They keep their equanimity and are even braced by the unsettling revelation that the subject has no place in the world; its place is to be without place.

This is what makes the dandy such an exemplary observer, of itself and of society: its sympathies do not lie with the person. A point that Virginia Woolf conveys comically when she notes: "If a man and a dog were drowning in the same pond [Brummel] would prefer to save the dog if there was nobody looking. But he was still persuaded that everybody was looking."[48] If the dandy's sympathies lie with the drowning dog, it is not from sentiment but misanthropy:[49] "I am Misanthropos, and hate mankind / For thy part, I do wish thou wert a dog, / that I might love thee something."[50] There is more than a little Timon of Athens in the dandy's sensibility: "Hate all, curse all, show charity to none, / But let the famished flesh slide from the bone / Ere thou relieve the beggar. Give to dogs / What thou deniest to men."[51] The dandy, like Timon, despises humanity's attachment to money: "Let molten coin be thy damnation."[52] In a famous anecdote, a beggar asks Brummel "for alms—'if only a halfpenny'. 'Poor fellow,' Brummel replied. 'I have heard of such a coin but never possessed one'; and gave him a shilling."[53]

CHAPTER 7

THE HAPPY MELANCHOLIC

The books that we need, to paraphrase Kafka,[1] remain those that bring us to a standstill, those posing a mute obstacle whose immobility cannot be grasped or evaded and whose apprehension comes at the cost of breaking the subject in two. Such broken subjects enter "the melancholy realm of eternal drizzle,"[2] a parallel world divested of hope, neither above nor below, but at the absent center of the world in which we live. The light that is shed from this center is black; the gaze illuminated by this black sun is melancholic.

Gérard de Nerval—to whom we owe the image of a black sun—remarks almost humorously, "[Melancholic hypochondria] is a terrible affliction—it makes one see things as they are."[3] In the melancholic's suffering, the cruelty of the real, to adopt Rosset's formula, asserts itself irremediably: the real, without ornament, stripped of sense, indigestible (*crudus*).[4] That which melancholia lays bare, this mute and oppressive obstacle, the *thing*, marks the separation of *objects* from their meaning. The melancholic inhabits an in-between state, where meaning as such is withdrawn. Signification becomes merely ornamental and language loses its grip on the real. Finding nothing in the world to activate its energies, the melancholic suffers from world-weariness, *taedium vitae* or *ennui*—what Baudelaire, the prince of melancholics, will transform into spleen.

The pathetic heroism of the melancholic lies in this subject's attempt to assume the void, and melancholia is the pathos of the subject's disjunction: the peculiar feeling of the *becoming object* of the subject. Absorbed by the void, the melancholic adopts the posture of the brooder whose contemplative gaze falls on *things* whose sheer indifference solicits no concern.[5] Compelled by the negativity of his own affect, the melancholic enters a circuit that passes from absence to absence: from a world deprived of substance to a subject lacking integrity to the null void that would seem to be their neutral and impartial sovereign.

To sketch the theoretical portrait of the melancholic requires tracing the structural space of the void's migration: from the object to the subject to the void in culture that marks their vertiginous superimposition. One might expect the portrait to be gloomy. Morbidity has been one of the melancholic's most persistent features. Yet the image that I would like here to invoke is that of a happy melancholic, a strange breed modeled more on the laughing than the weeping philosopher. The physiognomy of the melancholic may indeed be redolent with doom, but he shoulders this burden with an elegant nonchalance, finding a fitting phantasm for the dereliction of things.

****

Melancholia is the affective registration of the dereliction of things. By the dereliction of things, I mean the generalized rupture between objects and their significations that is inscribed into the heart of things by the commodity form. Benjamin writes, "The devaluation of the world of things in allegory is surpassed within the world of things itself by the commodity."[6] If baroque culture situated the void in the world—devaluing the world through its separation of things from their significations—modernity is the devaluation of spirit, of subjectivity, configuring a world that offers its subjects no refuge at all. The subject is offered no refuge since transcendence is inscribed into the world of things itself as the very operation that devalues them. Heaven becomes hell; one's salvation becomes bound to this world of things, whose transcendent promise is belied as a perpetual damnation. The baroque allegory of the world's mortal insignificance becomes crushingly literal, since through the social necessity of their exchange things themselves seem to perform their own evacuation, and the void that is left is offered to the subject as the sole means of its salvation. This void is effectively inscribed into things themselves, since as commodities they internalize through the function of exchange a relation to what they are not, and their value is the concealed expression of this negation. Incarnating the abstraction of their own value, commodities are constitutively outside of themselves. The thing can only proffer its own abstraction, its separation from itself, its own void, as the promise of a value that is structurally unattainable for a subject that is nonetheless socially committed to its reproduction. In this respect, melancholia registers affectively the thing's separation from itself, its abstraction, marking the subject with the void of its significance.

Melancholia is the disposition due to the exposure to the void: the event of this crushing abstraction. The danger of this disposition consists in the melancholic's peculiar response to this dereliction: to counter the void with the void, abstraction with abstraction.

Such a response seems to be profoundly empty, to such a degree that the melancholic would appear to succumb to that most romantic of affects, despair, finding himself overwhelmed by his inability to make sense, which is to say, to differentiate, to hold apart, to parse; in short, the ability to maintain the difference between the sign and its signification. Suicide is the persistent danger that afflicts this disposition of the mind: the desire, heroically exemplified by Hölderlin's Empedocles, to merge with the abyss, to plunge into the volcano, to disappear without a trace.[7] This is what links melancholia to depression. And for less heroic subjects, there is perhaps a fate worse than death, which Kristeva describes as a feeling of being dead without necessarily wanting to die. Suicide seems unnecessary, beside the point, since one feels already dead. This state of absolute apathy, of near-total dissociation from things, the world, the self, places the melancholic into a null, empty, hollow space, which Kristeva describes, following the speech of her patient Helen, as "an absolute, mineral, astral numbness, which was nevertheless accompanied by the impression, also an almost physical one, that this 'being dead,' physical and sensory as it might be, was also a thought nebula, an amorphous imagination, a muddled representation of some implacable helplessness. The reality and fiction of death's being. Cadaverization and artifice."[8] Overwhelmed with the loss of her subjectivity, her inability to differentiate herself from the void whose function places the subject into meaningful relation with things, the depressed melancholic succumbs. She succumbs to her own failure, to her own inability, to allude to Deleuze, to make a difference that makes a difference. One void comes crashing into the next.

The melancholic suffers what Fitzgerald describes as a "blow from within." This is not necessarily a dramatic blow, "the big sudden blows that come, or seem to come, from outside—the ones you remember and blame things on and, in moments of weakness, tell your friends about." He continues, "There is another sort of blow that comes from within—that you don't feel till it's too late to do anything about it, until you realize with finality that in some regard you will never be as good a man again."[9] The melancholic is the one who cracks; or perhaps the appropriate metaphor is that of a puncture, a slow wheezing leak that saps the subject of its vitality: "every act of life from the morning tooth-brush to the friend at dinner [becomes] an effort."[10]

In this case, worse than suicide is the hardening that takes place, the cynicism that Fitzgerald describes with a self-punishing lucidity. The cultivation of a voice calculated to "show no ring of conviction except the conviction of the person" one is talking to.

> And a smile—ah, I would get me a smile. I'm still working on that smile. It is to combine the best qualities of a hotel manager, an experienced old social weasel, a head-master on visitors' day, a colored elevator man, a pansy pulling a profile, a producer getting stuff at half its market value, a trained nurse coming on a new job, a body-vender in her first rotogravure,

a hopeful extra swept near the camera, a ballet dancer with an infected toe, and of course the great beam of loving kindness common to all those from Washington to Beverly Hills who must exist by virtue of the contorted pan.[11]

Cynicism in the end is nothing more than a will to correctness. Thus the devastating concluding line of "The Crack-Up": "I will try to be a correct animal though, and if you throw me a bone with enough meat on it I may even lick your hand."[12]

If these responses—suicide, dissociation, and cynicism—each mark a kind of terminal misery, what they share is the melancholic's incapacity to differentiate void from void, *a becoming melancholic about melancholy*. The problem thus becomes: How to avoid not identifying with the object of one's horror, the loss that threatens to engulf one's whole being? How to be evacuated without feeling utterly vacuous? How to prevent the melancholic's "self-immolation" from becoming "sodden-dark"? How to be open to the dereliction of things, to the demolition of their substance wrought by capital, without being destroyed by it: a suicide or an empty shell of a person?

This statement of the problem, doubtless, shares much with Deleuze's formulation: "how are we to stay at the surface without staying on the shore?"[13] Just as Deleuze speaks of the possibility of becoming a little schizophrenic, a little alcoholic, etc., knowing full well the ridiculousness of such propositions, can we speak of becoming a little melancholic, just enough to evacuate the world of its formal stability without becoming vacuous? If melancholia is the affective registration of the void's event, the problem concerns how to maintain a relation to it without being pathologically crippled by it; how to differentiate the void as event from *the place of the void* that swallows it. This distinction between the event and its place is nothing else than the effort of thought to differentiate itself from the feeling that engenders it. Thus the act of this separation is nothing less than the attempt to objectify the void, to gain the requisite distance so that the thinker is not crushed under its weight.

****

The act of separation is the indispensable function of the imagination. It is the phantasm that serves to separate the event of the void from its place. The melancholic's relation to the phantasm is the subject of Agamben's recondite analysis in one of his earliest books, *Stanzas: On Word and Phantasm in Western Culture*. The problem at the heart of this book—inventively taking up a legacy indebted as much to Martin Heidegger as to Walter Benjamin—concerns the manner in which the melancholic through his imagination internalizes a relation to the void, joyously occupying the null center of a parallel world, closer to the real because phantasmatic, illuminating the present through its radiant darkness. This image of radiant darkness, of a black sun, cuts to the heart of the "immobile dialectic" that structures the melancholic's relation to the void. The phantasm provides the subject with an image of its own deformation, making an object, so to speak, of its own disjunction. The phantasm is the disjunctive synthesis of two voids.

Agamben recasts the problem as it is posed by Freud in "Mourning and Melancholia" in terms informed by the medieval and Renaissance conception of black bile (*melaina chole*), the melancholic humor. Situating Freud within the intellectual landscape of the Renaissance enables Agamben to draw out a latent theory of the imagination, and thus of the phantasm, implied, but for the most part undeveloped, within Freud's psychoanalytic thought. Although it is at times obscure, this allows Agamben to extract a dialectical theory of the melancholic subject's imaginary relation to the real. The image (the phantasm) that defines melancholic desire (and hence its relation to itself and its world) does not play a mediating role but marks, rather, the site of a violent disjunction between desire (*eros*) and its "object." This gap between desire and itself defines the place (*topos*) of the image as the null space *between* the real and the unreal. Agamben thus defines culture as the space of this disjunction: "The topology of the unreal that melancholy designs in its immobile dialectic is, at the same time, a topology of culture."[14]

The phantasm then carves out a hollow space that makes possible an appropriation of absence itself (the void) in the form of an object. Following intuitions of Hölderlin and Rilke, whose epigraphs serve to frame the discussion of melancholia,[15] Agamben conceives of loss as the completion or affirmation of what is possessed, such that one possesses something only insofar as one loses it (whether the loss be actual or potential). Loss then expresses a joy in having lost, since loss is its condition of possibility. In this respect, melancholia has nothing to do with a nostalgic fixation on the past. On the contrary, the melancholic's fixation on negativity is the condition for having done with possession, a condition for finding a certain joy inseparable from pain in dispossession.

The crux of Agamben's position can be most clearly discerned in his reading of Freud's essay "On Mourning and Melancholia." Following the work of Karl Abraham, Freud begins by marking a similarity between mourning and melancholia—the fact that like the aggrieved, the melancholic suffers from "a profoundly painful dejection, abrogation of interest in the outside world, loss of the capacity to love, inhibition of all activity."[16] However, whereas mourning always concerns the loss of a determinate object, whether real (a loved one or object) or ideal (a notion), melancholia is *at a loss*, so to speak, as to *what* it is that has been lost. Since *what* is lost is not given in melancholia but remains unconscious, the loss, Freud argues, is a relation to an object that has been *introjected* and thus appears as a lack in the subject. As Freud puts it, the "loss of the object" becomes "transformed into a loss in the ego."[17] And it is this emptying out of the subject—"an impoverishment of [the melancholic's] ego on a grand scale"[18]—that accounts for the self-loathing of the melancholic: the key symptom that does not appear in grief. "In grief the world becomes poor and empty; in melancholia it is the ego itself."[19]

This lack in the ego, Agamben stresses, is a relation to a loss that is original and not derivative, as is the case in mourning. In melancholia, the loss that precedes the loss of an object and thus the withdrawal of the libido itself is "the original datum." Unlike mourning that responds to the event of a lost object, melancholia responds to the event of loss as such: an absence that cannot be made present. What has been lost is some thing that precedes the very constitution of the subject (as a relation to objects) and whose absence is irreparable. As such, "melancholia offers the paradox of an intention to mourn that precedes and anticipates the loss of the object."[20] In Agamben's interpretation, melancholia is the ontological ground of mourning. There is some thing that obtrudes in melancholia—a symptom—that cannot be derived from the subject's relation to objects. It is not the object but the subject's *relation to* the object that is exposed in melancholia. What makes itself felt in melancholia is a relation to that which is nonobjective in the subject: the feeling of absence as such.

The subject relates to this space through a lack, a difference, that is felt and precedes the difference between the subject and the object—what Heidegger would no doubt call the ontological difference. Strangely, melancholia makes mourning possible in a situation where there is nothing to be mourned, since there is no object that has been lost. Drawing on his reading of *acedia*, Agamben thus concludes "that the withdrawal of melancholic libido has no other purpose than to make viable an appropriation in a situation in which none is really possible. From this point of view, melancholy would be not so much the regressive reaction to the loss of the love object as the imaginative capacity to make an unobtainable object appear as if lost."[21] The imagination is that which makes the negative manifest *as if it were* an object.

By drawing out the latent ontological background of Agamben's interpretation, we can see that the imagination is the faculty that places the subject into a relation with that which is not. Something new can come into being only if it appears as something already lost. Melancholia is the creative genius of making *nothing* appear. Melancholia is the appropriation of negativity. The object that melancholia bestows with funereal trappings is the *nothing* as such: the void. The void has to appear as if it were lost in order to be found, and the image is the site of this paradoxical reversal. This structure belies the perversity of the imagination that relates nothing to something in order to make something out of nothing. The nothing names a loss that cannot be lost because it is possessed as loss. Vice versa it cannot be possessed because, as a possession of loss, it is dispossessed of possession. This demented and maniacal reversal, this turning within the void, which can be thought only at the risk of reducing thought to this kind of non-sense, secures for the nothing an *absolute* place.

The fact that the void can appear only as *that which it is not* entails that it can only lay claim to a simulated existence. The nothing, the void, is defined as the existence of the unreal, the very place where *that which is not* can come into being. The peculiar labor of the imagination, then, consists in inscribing negativity into reality: seizing the void. That which is lost and at the same time found through the very appropriation of loss, is the phantasm: "The imaginary loss that so obsessively occupies the melancholic tendency has no real object, because its funereal strategy is directed to the impossible capture of the phantasm."[22] The phantasm here is not an image of something, but precisely the imprint of an absence which can only have a simulated presence. Conversely, the presence of the phantasm merely attests to an absence. By means of the phantasm, the "real loses its reality so that what is unreal may become real."[23] This gap, this disjunction within the phantasm itself, is that which brings the melancholic to a standstill at the same time as it makes novelty real Melancholia is the sickness born of creativity whose emblem is Dürer's melancholic angel.

The phantasm, as it is here conceived, does not play a mediating role. It is not a synthesis of presence and absence unless one is to speak of a disjunctive synthesis. The phantasm provides a minimal consistency to the void (absence) necessary for sustaining the subject's attachment to the reality of objects. Yet at the same time, the grip that this reality has on the subject, its power to convict, is loosened. The subject is neither wholly withdrawn from reality (schizophrenia) nor convinced by its normative appeal. The phantasm's fiction serves to divide the subject without necessitating its destruction. The subject is disjunctively synthesized through its phantasmatic objectification. Put differently, the phantasm is the objectification of the split in the subject. The melancholic "*identification* of the ego with the abandoned object,"[24] to quote Freud, is in fact an attachment to the phantasm that presents a (subjective) loss in objective form. The phantasm is the objectifcation of an absence, the void's phantasmagorical presence. The reflexive nature of melancholia consists in the subject's becoming object—a will toward self-objectification. It is this morose attachment to his own absence that becomes the melancholic's dearest, most prized possession—the paradoxical possession through his objectification of his own dispossession. The melancholic is an absentee subject, the phantasm, the placeholder of the void.

The phantasm is neither a delusion nor an illusion. It neither suppresses nor conceals reality. Rather it exhibits reality's deformation. It perverts reality in the Freudian sense that it neither negates (*verneint*) nor affirms the given. It is rather a disavowal (*Verleugnung*) of reality. The melancholic becomes a fetishist. Agamben, like Kristeva, links the structure of melancholia to fetishism. For Freud, the fetish relates to the child's own encounter with its own lack, namely the anxiety of castration and its revelation of insufficiency. Confronted with the revelation of the void, the fetishist disavows it. The disavowal of the void entails attaching it to something, an object, that neither fills it in, takes its place, nor reproduces it. Paradoxically, the fetish presents an absence. The fetish becomes a sign of the void *and* of its absence. The fetish binds the void to an object by localizing their disjunction, immobilizing it. The fetish, like the melancholic phantasm, is a disjunctive synthesis. Agamben can thus maintain: "Similarly, in melancholia the object is neither appropriated nor lost, but both possessed and lost at the same time. And as the fetish is at once the sign of something and its absence, and owes to this contradiction its own phantomatic status, so the object of the melancholic project is at once real and unreal, incorporated and lost, affirmed and denied."[25] Both the fetish and the phantasm mark an objectification of a splitting that is internalized by the sign that refers the subject to its own incompleteness (its not-wholeness).

Kristeva develops this aspect of the melancholic fetish at length. "Everywhere denial [*Verleugnung*] effects splittings and devitalizes representations and behaviours as well."[26] The melancholic maintains the sign's division and evacuates its meaning. This evacuation becomes an image of the subject's own splitting that distances the subject from meaning by distancing the sign from its signification.[27] This is what Benjamin had already identified as the "majesty of the allegorical intention: to destroy the organic and the living—to eradicate semblance [*Schein*]."[28] In the fetish, the phantasm is mobilized against *Schein*, for what appears is the relation to that which is not, as if the *act* of appearing served to evacuate the appearance itself. The melancholic phantasm immobilizes this act, as if the subject encountered a kink in reality that brought it to a standstill by shocking it with an image of itself. Culture is the place where the melancholic encounters his own absence: this epiphany of the void, the no-man's-land staked out by the phantasm's objective seizure of the subject's absence.

****

The phantasmatic seizure of the void's event as objectification of the subject's dissolution becomes with Baudelaire a condition of artistic practice. Spleen is the phantasmatic foundation of his poetic enterprise. Spleen functions as an intoxicant. By allowing himself to imbibe it liberally, he establishes a certain stability to his practice, as if drinking himself sober. For spleen is a phantasm that brings focus to a sensibility that is otherwise woefully manic, lending to his rage the lucidity requisite "to break into the world, to lay waste its harmonious structures."[29] By making his melancholia a poetic constant, Baudelaire makes the objectification of the void the center of his reflexive labor.

Traversing the landscape of melancholia, Baudelaire consigns his subjectivity to the spleen, to that melancholic organ that sends "gross fumes into the brain, and so *per consequens* disturbing the soul, and all the faculties of it."[30] The focal image of his enterprise, spleen is at once object and subject of Baudelaire's poetry: that which speaks in the subject and that about which the subject speaks. As speaking and spoken, spleen is an image that marks a space between the subject and object, the collision, so to speak, of their respective voids. Spleen as poetic utterance—posited as the object seized and laid bare by the word—is no longer simply an expressive lament (a confession of world-weariness), but, qua spleen, it actively marks the distance of the subject from itself, creating that necessary hollow where the subject can announce its own absence.

This is perhaps what Benjamin means when he writes, "The decisively new ferment that enters the *taedium vitae* and turns it into spleen is self-estrangement. In Baudelaire's melancholy [*Trauen*], all that is left of the infinite regress of reflection—which in Romanticism playfully expanded the space of life into ever wider circles and reduced it within ever narrower frames—is the 'somber and lucid *tête-à-tête*' of the subject with itself."[31] In turning back on itself, the I encounters its own radical dissociation. Baudelaire strips or lays bare the romantic reflexive operation, shifting the accent from the identity to the nonidentity of the I. Through the spleen's disjunctive synthesis, the I enters into a relation with itself, but it encounters its "self" as a nonidentity, for its very identity consists in spleen. If spleen conditions the subject's objectification, then its separation from itself, from the life within, becomes what is most native to it, what is most its own; its very impropriety becomes what is most proper to it. What speaks in the poem and what is spoken is alienation: a lyrical I estranged from itself.

Spleen provides Baudelaire with an image of the I that decomposes in its composition, a snapshot of the I's objectification. Through a poetic image, spleen, the I is placed into an ex-centric relation with itself by its identification with the object, the spleen (at once affect and organ) that tempers it. Spleen is the organ, the poetic machine within the body of the text that produces the I as atra-bilious. Objectified in the spleen, the I is produced as estranged; rather than resolving, it dissolves the consistency of the I, making the moment of enunciation, the saying of "I," the enunciation of a part, the spleen, that dissolves the whole. This contradiction serves to divide the I, as if forcing it to coincide with its own disjunction. The I manages to stage itself through the poem only as disjunct, disintegrated. Through this process of identification with the spleen, the I becomes a placeholder of its own absence: "I am a graveyard that the moon abhors / where long worms like regrets come out to feed / most ravenously on me dearest dead. / I am an old boudoir where a rack of gowns, / perfumed by withered roses, rots to dust ..."[32]

As Baudelaire opens his last, unfinished project for an autobiographical poem, "My Heart Laid Bare," "Of the vaporization and centralization of the self. Everything is here." The withdrawal into the I is the condition of its vaporization. The construction of the poem enacts this dual operation: centralization and vaporization. The poem is the condition for the emergence of an I that is vapor, a sensible mist or the mist of a sensibility that engulfs the language of the poem, giving it atmosphere. Yet this ideality of vaporization is always placed into relation with a counterimage that decomposes the ideal. Spleen and ideal have to be read as an immobile dialectic in which the idealization of spleen is offset by the spleenification of the ideal.

In the first poem of *Paris Spleen*, "The Stranger," this "enigmatic man" without father, mother, brother, or sister, without family or country, this figure without origin or place is the I that loves and hates: an I that could love beauty, hates gold, but above all loves the clouds, "the clouds that pass ... up there ... up there ... the wonderful clouds."[33] A formulation that drifts like the image it invokes. The clouds in their billowing drift are the very phantasm of elegant deformation. If this is the extremity of the idealization of spleen (idealization of deformation), the logic of Baudelaire's practice is to produce a kink in the ideal: "their nebulous shapes become / a splendid hearse for my dreams, / their red glow the reflection / of the Hell where my heart's at home."[34] The cloud become hearse is the vehicle that carries the corpse to its tomb. The corpse is the cloud's violation (the spleenification of the ideal), the rotting corpse as the eminently inelegant reminder of what awaits the substrate of all human ideals. And Baudelaire's dandyism prescribes that he is to become an elegant corpse, a rotting ideal.[35]

The corpse provides the I with the image of an identity that coincides with its most radical decomposition. The poetic image occasions the seizure of a subjective destitution as radical as it is irreparable: "My soul is cracked, and when in distress / it tries to sing the chilly nights away, / how often its enfeebled voice suggests / the gasping of a wounded soldier left / beside a lake of blood, who, pinned beneath / a pile of dead men, struggles, stares and dies."[36] And yet it is precisely in this seizure that the happiness of the melancholic lies.

The fantasy of the melancholic is to be a happy corpse. As Baudelaire asserts in "The Happy Corpse,"[37] this most bleak and humorous of poems, for a corpse to be happy it is not sufficient for the body to be consigned to the grave, deprived of life and lying in wait for the officialdom of mourning. The happiness of the corpse does not lie in death but in digestion. It is when the corpse is ingested by those "scions of decay," those "feasting philosophers,"[37] the worms, that it is happy. Only when reduced to bone, picked clean by contracted crows, does it rest content. It is only when reduced to its skeletal architecture that it can sleep in peace, "like a shark in the cradling wave." This would be the fantasy of a "soulless body deader than the dead." A body deprived of soul longs to be restored to the inorganic, insensate matter. To be deader than the dead is to be extinct, a bone awaiting fossilization. In short, the melancholic desires to be an object whose psychic life has been effaced, subtracted irreparably from the very vicissitudes of sensate flesh that provide the conditions and thus torments of psychic life. "From the perspective of spleen," it is not simply "the buried man," as Benjamin suggests, that 'is the 'transcendental subject' of historical consciousness"; it is the corpse picked clean.[38] It is not in awaiting, but being deprived of, a second life that the melancholic locates its joy, and this is what binds the melancholic to evil.

To see the corpse from the inside[39] is to become the impersonator of bone, the mask of a fossilized presence. The subject is inserted into culture only through the maximization of its distance from the organic. Culture thus becomes a space that is beyond decay, since it marks what cannot die. If the happiness of the melancholic lies in its phantasmatic identification with its own extinction, this is because at this hyperbolic extreme what is most heavy becomes bearably light, and the void that crushes becomes the void whose phantasmatic seizure marks this thinking animal's commitment to a culture that praises something other than stupefaction.

CONCLUSION

A HOLE IN A THING IT IS NOT

There are at least two ways of leaving a trace, a mark, let us say, a footprint in the snow. There is that of Good King Wenceslas, the righteous king (*rex justus*), the pious master, who leaves footsteps in the snow for his ailing page to follow. As John Mason Neale's carol from 1853 puts it: "'Mark my footsteps, good my page. Tread thou in them boldly / Thou shalt find the winter's rage freeze thy blood less coldly.' / In his master's steps he trod, where the snow lay dinted; / Heat was in the very sod which the saint had printed." And there is, on the contrary, the footprints that Danny leaves, or better, does not leave, for his demented father, played, of course, by Jack Nicholson, in Stanley Kubrick's *The Shining*.

At stake in this opposition between these two footprints is not simply a distinction between a sign that leads and one that misleads, between the true and the false, but the differing manners in which these signs, these footprints, serve to inscribe the subject's relation to the markers of its appearance, the signs of its legibility. For Wenceslas imprints his footstep, so the legend goes, with a sign of his saintly character. It is the presence of warmth, this physical manifestation of his spiritual beneficence, that establishes a relation between the objectivity of his physical absence and the quality of his spiritual presence. By following his master's footsteps, the page's weakening physical being is strengthened by the trace presence of his master's spiritual being, whose traces mark a path not simply to the hearth but to heaven itself.

For Danny the problem is the opposite. Faced with the impossible task of having to efface all traces of his physical being, he assumes, through a repetition of his own lack in/of place, the void of his presence. The act of retracing his footsteps, adopting the very imprint of his absence, radicalizes the split between his footprint qua sign of his physical presence (an indicator of his place) and the sign's physical presence as a marker of absence. Assuming his sign's objective character of lack, Danny internalizes the difference between his footprint as a sign of his present *absence* and the footprint as a sign of his absent *presence*. It is the act of repetition that serves to differentiate the sign's divisive power from its signifying or indicative function: the manner in which it bores a hole into the snowy plain and as consequence leaves a trace of his presence that indicates his direction.

Wenceslas's footprints cannot lead his page astray. Their retention of warmth, a sign of the good, grounds their direction in truth. Those who follow will find the way to hearth and home and ultimately to heaven above. These signs thus serve the symbolic function of *protecting* the place and right of kingship, as well as supporting the belief in a world in which a sign's truth receives its proper measure from the beneficent. The faithful page lives in a world where one has confidence in one's betters, trusts in their humanity, and where the subject knows its place. One just has to follow the signs. In such a world, prudence would indeed follow Emerson's maxim: "Trust men, and they will be true to you; treat them greatly, and they will show themselves great, though they make an exception in your favor to all their rules of trade."[1]

But Melville knew better. "God help the poor fellow," he notes with reference to Emerson's advice, "who squares his life according to this."[2] Danny's world is one in which fathers, like kings, having lost all sense of measure, can only maintain their authority by devouring their children. This Titanic world is one of consummate horror, where the least sign of a subject's appearance, Danny's footsteps, marks one for death. Unable to efface his traces without, in turn, being effaced, Danny finds an ingenious solution: actively unhinging the sign from its signifying function—untethering it from all sense of propriety—turning the very marking of his place to his advantage. Like the confidence man, Danny makes use of the sign's leading quality to mislead.

Danny escapes from the destructive logic of his trace—the way in which it marks him for death—only by assuming the signs of his presence as the very markers of his absence. Assuming his footprint not simply as a sign of his presence but the very cut (a void in the snow) that marks his relation to absence, Danny *impersonates* the signs of his own absence. To retrace his footsteps, to count them again in reverse, he must *proceed negatively*, he must be able to count the manner in which he counts for nothing. He counts himself out. Presenting himself as absent, Danny misleads neither by leaving a false trace nor by simply effacing his tracks in the snow, as a cat covers its shit, but hides them in place by retracing, remarking, registering, that is to say, *repeating* them, as if to absent himself in place.

The illusion of his disappearance lies in making a footprint that is not a footprint by being a footprint.[3] A logical riddle that Danny indeed solves by walking backward in the very dint of his own tread: repeating not simply the footprint but its *character of lack*. By doing so, Danny differentiates the sign's referential function (i.e., the sign's capacity to present what is absent) from the mere fact of its inscription. He registers the difference between the imprint (the fact of inscription) and its sense: shifting the stress from the *presentation* of absence to the presentation of *absence*: from absent presence to present absence. A slight, imperceptible shift, as if passing from void to void (to recall M. Teste: dandy and nihilist), that has miraculous effects. By repeating the sign of his absent presence as an empty act of inscription, what is *registered* is his present absence.

This act of repetition differentiates the footprint *as a hole in a thing it is not* from its referential function as a sign that indicates the direction of his person. Danny *makes something* ... he makes something vanish, namely the presence of his person. It is his capacity to repeat the empty place of the sign (the *sculptural* act that *objectifies* his presence) by registering it that allows him to appear to disappear. Proceeding negatively, repeating the place of his absence, Danny makes an object of his absence. He objectifies the void.

By relating to the sign that marks the absence of his presence *as an absence*, Danny can mislead precisely by leading, that is, by leading his father to his absence. Like a magician, he makes his person vanish. Positioning the sign within the space of its own inconsistency—where it at once leads *and* misleads, is true *and* false—Danny hides the signifying power of his trace by repeating it, occupying the difference between his footprint's signification (an absence that refers to a presence) and its pure form (the presentation of an absence). He positions himself in the place of his own absence: the empty footprint, the void of his presence.

Danny thus inhabits the gap within signification that is constituted by the act of repetition itself. The fact that the presentation of an absence enables one to hide a presence through a repetition of the act of registration indicates a difference between that which is repeated (the imprint) and the act of repetition itself (the act of imprinting). This structural difference between repetition (that which is repeated) and the act, between the place and an act that takes place, entails that signification is always already divided. The repetition of an act divides the act differentiating the place from the place that the mark occupies. Repetition reinscribes through the registration of absence a difference between the material event of the sign, the act of its taking place, and the advent of its signification.

It is this difference that Lacan highlights when he maintains: "the realization of the signifier will never be able to be careful enough in its memorization to succeed in designating the primacy of the significance as such."[4] The act of inscription (the realization of the signifier) divides the real, marking the space of a cut (a division, a gap) that can only be repeated, since its act evades designation. What is designated by means of repetition is the place of signification, but not the act that introduces absence into the real. That which can only be repeated is paradoxically that which is not repeatable, for repetition names something that repeats (anything whatever), and yet, on the other hand, that thing which is repeated has to be differentiated from the act of repetition as such, which is nonidentical with the thing, concept, word, etc. that is repeated. Repetition divides itself between the act and what it makes possible, namely the repeatable.

Repetition as the act of repeating is nonidentical with that which is repeated. And this leads to an interesting paradox of repetition, namely that *what is repeated* is repeatable, but the *act* of repetition itself is unrepeatable. One cannot repeat the act of repetition, only the thing repeated. The paradox of repetition's sense can be posed as follows: to repeat repetition is to repeat the unrepeatable. "Repetition," as Lacan puts it, "demands the new."[5] That which is new is the absence, which as such is unrepeatable: the hole that is punched by the placing of the sign. This paradox results in the tendency for the act of repetition to divide itself from that upon which repetition depends, which is always something other than repetition, namely, that which is repeatable. Thus repetition repeats the unrepeatable.

Furthermore, repetition of the act enacts the liquidation of its sense. Each act of repetition involves the *whole* of repetition, including through its act that which is unrepeatable. Repetition is nothing but this splitting of itself and thus the very *sense* of the whole, since it becomes identified with its act. Repetition, as at once part *and* whole, names this identification with its own nonsense. A whole and a part is a whole that is not. This disjunctive synthesis of an opposition unhinges the sense of the whole by including it in what it is not, a single act (a part). Repetition repeats this internal division that makes possible the distinction between that which takes place (the act of repetition) and the place of taking place (the repeatable).

In retracing his footsteps, Danny does not repeat himself, but relates to the act of repetition that divides his appearance between its place (the act of placing that makes a void) and the sign's occupation of that place: a difference between the presence of the foot (even qua absent) and the hollow it makes in the snow (the void of its presence). The sign becomes a sign of its own absence through a repetition of the sign's indicative function, situating it in the place of its own absence, repeating the manner in which it indicates the place of Danny's presence. The sign must lead in order to mislead; it thus leads *and* therefore misleads. In effect, by relating to the act of repetition Danny separates himself from himself, the place of subject from the person that appears in its place, by separating the lack (the void in place) from *what* is lacking (the presence toward which the absence points). To repeat, to *proceed negatively*, is not merely a matter of going in reverse, like playing a film backward. The thinking required to repeat an act relates to the disjunction between the forward and the backward. The backward repeats the forward and thereby misleads by leading. What is marked or registered through the act of repetition is the footprint *as thing*, i.e., as a hole in a thing it is not. By identifying with this gap—this object-void—occupying the site of a repeated footprint, Danny identifies with that character of absence that assigns to him his lack of character. Becoming the impersonator of his own absence, Danny is what I have been calling an absentee subject. To be an absentee subject, it is not enough to simply efface one's traces; one has to repeat the absence they make, positioning the subject in the object place of its absence

This formula—*a thing is a hole in a thing it is not*—I borrow from a statement by the sculptor Carl Andre.[6] The place of the subject is positioned in relation to the difference between the hole that is made in space and the space of the hole, a difference the subject maintains only through the object of its attachment. The subject is attached to the thing as hole. If Danny sustains this difference through the act of repetition, it is because through this act he *makes* an object of his absence. Danny is a sculptor. He shines. He has the sixth sense.

****

If Danny is a sculptor, it is because he *relates to* the absence he makes. A sculptor thus need not make anything. It is only necessary that one make nothing. Like a poet (from *poiein*: to make), to borrow W. H. Auden's formula, the sculptor makes nothing happen. In making *something*, whatever it may be or become, the sculptor makes a hole. Nothing is always made, in addition to whatever is made.

If I opened this study of the absentee subject, as the subject of disorientation, with a consideration of Duchamp as a thinker whose thought is inseparable from the apparatus he constructs, it was to assert the novel hole he makes. He makes a hole into which art itself is then placed. Duchamp's readymade is a paradigmatic case of making in this sense, regardless of how he himself may have understood it. The readymade is obviously something, but its function establishes art within a generic space by making a hole with art. As *not not-art*, I tried to show, the readymade's in-difference is not simply a double negation, but something like a hole in art. A form of thinking about art practice that is a result of the decision to not make something but to make nothing (the thing was ready-made) and to place what was made, namely the void. The readymade becomes a matter of placing, with all the consequent problems that accrue to this new problem. In placing the readymade, Duchamp does not take the space as given; he makes the place for it, *generically* speaking, so that the hole that he's made, no matter how slight or infrathin, becomes discernible. Art then is that thing, which is a hole, or, better, makes a hole in given sense for a subject summoned to think the nothing that happened. A hole is a thing in a hole it is not.

This is not a formula that Duchamp himself uttered. Rather he had it coined. In the image that Duchamp used for the cover of the International Collectors Society sales brochure (1967), Duchamp shows himself smoking a cigar, prominently displaying in his left hand a coinlike medallion that looks a lot like one of his last assisted readymades, *Drain Stopper (Bouche-évier)* (1964), but is likely the medal for the *Marcel Duchamp Art Medal*, which is indeed based on *Drain Stopper*.[7] A hole is a thing in a hole it is not: *Drain Stopper* as a sculpture could not be more succinctly formulated.

Duchamp the subject, by basing the medal on *Drain Stopper*, could not be more clear: as a symbol whose function is to symbolize value, excellence, meaning in art, and whose *title* bears the name of Duchamp's *person* as its ground and guarantor, this symbol counts for nothing. Whatever value it may serve to generate will amount to nothing but an elaborate hoax, appealing, of course, to the human, all too human, need for idols and honors, as that crucial support that allows a person to say it is *not nothing*. Thus Duchamp forces a decision: one can either recognize the medal as a medal of value, a tangible guarantee that the artist, when all is said and done, is *not nothing*, or one can see the *not nothing* for what it in fact is: a drain stopper, a *bouche-évier*, a collector and decisive mediator whose function is to facilitate drainage.

A symbol, like a word, is a sieve whose sense is composed of the filth that does not simply pass but collects on its surface. A word is a clogged pore. The French title, *Bouche-évier* (literally referring to the hole or "mouth" of the sink), puns on the French word *bouche-trou*. Between *bouche-évier* and *bouche-trou* a host of senses proliferate: a lowly, ordinary object of great use if one wants to prevent the clogging of one's pipes; the hole in the sink itself; more colloquially, it is a stopgap, a substitute or surrogate, a replacement for lack of something better, the last thing one can use to plug up a hole, to fill a gap, a go-to device, ready to hand like spray foam; it also has the sense of being filler, a throw-away amusement, something senseless to amuse or dispel boredom, to while away a little time, to fill the space between 0 and 0; more literally, and altogether Beckettian, it is the mouth-hole (*bouche*: mouth and *trou*: hole or gap), the site of speech and consumption, not to mention the place where words themselves get eaten, where sense goes down the drain.

Drain Stopper puts all these senses into play. It is a truly comical object. It presents itself as an object-image of the drain of sense: the empty place of the signifier whose meaning is formed through the filling of its void—which is, after all, the use to which one puts a drain stopper: it fits into a hole; it catches debris. *Drain Stopper* provides as object an image of a hole that one inserts into a hole: a hole as thing in a hole it is not. This is the groundless ground upon which the *Duchamp Art Medal* is based. To believe and invest in its symbolic significance forces a perverse compromise: a betrayal of the non-sense of art for which Duchamp deeply and sincerely cared, namely the art that can make holes happen, that can make subjects *think*. Duchamp never abandons Julien Torma's aligning of thought and charlatanism:

> It is not *natural* to think: one must create a veritable stage-setting out of oneself and things, not to mention the inevitable artificial device of reasoning. ... Without these shams, thought is no more than naivete (banging on about the obvious) and, basically, stupidity. Intelligence involves deception as speech does lying.
>
> Better to admit frankly to this rule of the game and do knowingly what everyone else does unknowingly. Deliberately inject into one's thought the element of charlatanry required for it to be thought, rather than oneself be its dupe. In this way, one can vary the dosage *as one pleases*. Cagliostro was a thinker ...[8]

There is perhaps no better description of the *Duchamp Art Medal*. Duchamp was always willing to play the confidence man, nihilist, and dandy; the medal would be a final homage to the ridiculous, a monument to stupidity, a comical perversion of his concerns and legacy, and for that very reason, perhaps, a *fitting end*. Serving the *umouristic* function of turning his career as an artist into an elaborate and senseless joke that builds, like the *Aristocrats*, through elaborate profanation toward a deflationary end. A one-liner that falls flat: a joke without a punch line. Duchamp, like Beckett (albeit more aloof, less anguished, more nonchalant), borrowing Coetzee's description of the latter, "eventually settled on philosophical comedy as the medium for his uniquely anguished, arrogant, self-doubting, scrupulous temperament."[9]

****

Duchamp apprehends, like Danny, that the place of the object is a hole and that the most one can do is relate oneself to it by making an object of one's absence. Duchamp leaves a footprint in art. And like Danny, Duchamp plays with its duplicity. In the photograph in the brochure for the Collectors Society, Duchamp shows us his *Medal*, this signifier of his absence and the hole that he has made in art. As already mentioned, Duchamp himself from out of a thick cloud of cigar smoke does indeed appear to be absorbed in its contemplation; the medallion seems to magnetize his gaze as it does our own. Its rather peculiar manner of presentation makes us think of a hypnotist. As a symbol of his artistic achievement, the *Duchamp Medal* is, of course, an honor, but such honors only come at the end of a career, the end of a life. Although the medal recognizes the value of his artistic contribution, it also implies his imminent absence: an absence from which its symbolic value derives.

The *Medal* itself can only confer value through its attachment to Duchamp's *person*, becoming a symbol of his *absent presence*. Although those to whom he shows the medal in the photograph may indeed see this presence (its symbolic value), Duchamp qua subject, qua model, can only see a surrogate, a decoy, an imposter; he can only see his *present absence*. Is not the *Duchamp Medal*, like all "values," Duchamp asks with Nietzsche, just a decoy that prolongs "the comedy without ever getting closer to a denouement"?[10] As Duchamp doubtless understood, as an object of vanity the *Duchamp Medal* is at once a *vanitas*. Although it may show us the value of his absence, it can only serve to show Duchamp himself his own absence, his imminent end, and the place where all values go, not simply down the drain but into the grave. It presents to him the hole he already occupies.

The *Duchamp Medal* is a skull bone. In the end, we return, as does Duchamp, to the readymade as the bone of culture. Yet if Duchamp is a melancholic, he too, like Baudelaire, is happy. His illustrious art of living absently shows that "*continuing* with an 'In vain,' without aim and purpose," far from leading to *paralytic* thought, leads to the comic embrace of what could be indeed framed as a tragic insight: "when one realizes one's being fooled and yet has no power to prevent oneself being fooled."[11]

The fool is not a tragic but a comic figure. And only a fool would indeed treat a thing as a hole, to declare that something is nothing. Democritus, after all, is the laughing philosopher. Duchamp, for all his intellectual refinement, knew how to play the fool. To say that something is nothing by being something is foolish. When we relate to a footprint not as a sign of mastery but as a hole in the ground, something magical happens: the subject appears as absent. In this hole, the intelligent and the foolish meet. Like Dupin, whose name alludes to the dupe, Duchamp grasps that ratiocination is the art not simply of unmasking deception but of grasping its truth. Art is nothing if not the truth of deception. To say this is a sculpture that is not a sculpture by being a sculpture is to speak non-sense. It is to say this footprint is not a footprint by being a footprint. It is to say a thing is a hole in a thing it is not, or a hole is a thing in a hole it is not. The figure summoned by such non-sense cannot escape thinking its own absence. Positioned in the void, such a subject exhibits itself as the object of its absence. Like the sculptor, this subject makes an object of its absence.

Duchamp himself does this not simply with the *Duchamp Medal*, but above all with the play that he sets into motion in the brochure photograph. Duchamp shows us, as if through anamorphosis, what it is that he sees and what it is that we are to see by his seeing. Although it *appears* that Duchamp is looking at what we are looking at, namely the *Medal* he shows us, this is in fact impossible. The photograph functions like a magic trick that exhibits its own sleight of hand. Positioned in darkness, engulfed in cigar smoke, the very image of Lucifer—or is it Alistair Crowley?—Duchamp's obscure gaze emanates as if from a hole. We spectators are transfixed by what he shows—the *Medal*—and this hypnotic spell is only broken at a second glance, so to speak, when we notice that Duchamp cannot see the object he shows. The fact that he appears to see it is a photographic sleight of hand. Far from transfixed by the surface of *The Medal's* radiance, Duchamp's gaze, at this second glance, falls into the void, as if sucked into the black hole that devours the center of the image and whose vortex is marked by a turbulent swirl of cigar smoke. Duchamp in fact looks upon nothing: the void between his eye and the object. The object of *The Medal*, despite appearances, does not triangulate our respective points of view. Our respective gazes do not meet. And as if to stress both this perspectival illusion and its shattering, the actual object on which the lens itself is focused is Duchamp's face and perhaps even his eye: an eye, however, that is obscured, hidden by the smoke he is in the act of exhaling. Duchamp is blowing smoke in our eyes, blinding us just as the *Medal* itself blinds us to the hole it occupies.

For there is indeed another object in the photograph held poised and whose ash is directed at the picture plane, as if to burn a hole in its surface. This form of the hole, this *vitola*, repeats the circular form of the *Medal*, placed on the same horizontal axis. The photograph's composition establishes a formal relation of equivalency between cigar and *Medal*, the left and the right hand, as if Duchamp himself was taking the measure of these two objects on display, each competing for presence. Although the *Medal* at first takes pride of place, it is clearly the cigar that wins out, whose formless emissions take command of the tableau and fill it with their ominous meanderings.

The smoke itself doubtless reminds us of Duchamp's cover for *View* magazine (1945) depicting a bottle emitting smoke into the cosmic abyss and whose back cover contained the following definition of *infra-mince*: "Quand la fumée de tabac sent aussi de la bouche qui l'exhale, les deux odeurs s'épousent par infra-mince [When the smoke of tobacco also smells of the mouth which exhales it, the two smells are conjoined [literally, married] by the infra-thin]." On the brochure, Duchamp as his own substitute (*bouche-trou*) appears as the one emitting smoke. With the aid of his object—the cigar—he imbricates space (the void) with his present absence, filling it with a smoke that retains the trace imprint of Duchamp's own mouth cavity. The smoke that wafts in the direction of the *Duchamp Medal* based on *Bouche-évier* is blown from the hole of a mouth: that hole into which one plugs a cigar. It is not merely the art object, the *Duchamp Metal*, that is a substitute for Duchamp's presence; the stub of a cigar becomes an instrument for making Duchamp absent. If the cigar establishes one's identity—as Charles Dickens captured when he uttered: "Ah, if only I had brought a cigar with me! This would have established my identity"—it can also serve the function of making absent, hiding Duchamp's presence as the footstep occasions Danny's disappearance. The identity of Duchamp here at issue is not that of the name DUCHAMP which lends a symbolic identity and value to the *Medal* on display, but that other Duchamp whose identity is wagered on *infra-mince* (the less than thin). This present absence is marked by the hole that he holds aloft between his index and middle fingers. A better *bouche-trou* than *bouche-évier*, the cigar makes an object of Duchamp's absence. The stub is that eternal remainder stained by Duchamp's singular breath.

****

Sculpture makes an object of one's absence, locating oneself in the void that appears as a thing. Nobody has understood this better than Isa Genzken. Sculptures themselves are always self-portraits. Not strictly speaking of the visage, of the person of the sculptor, but of the meat of the brain (*Mein Gehirn*, 1984), the bone of the cranium, the jaw, the tooth (*X-Rays*, 1989–1991). These are not necessarily the works that garner a reputation or make a career, but, existing in the margins or cracks of a stupendous oeuvre, they serve as reminders that the effort of sculptural thinking strives to form some image, however vague or precise, of the nullity of the real. Genzken's *X-Ray* self-portraits are perhaps the most literal way to index the concern that I have pursued in the course of this book. The skull bone of the artist tipping a glass. In this ridiculous and dark image, bleak and relentlessly funny, we see the present absence of one trying with drink and/or art to loosen the skin of the person, to draw near to the heap of bones we are.

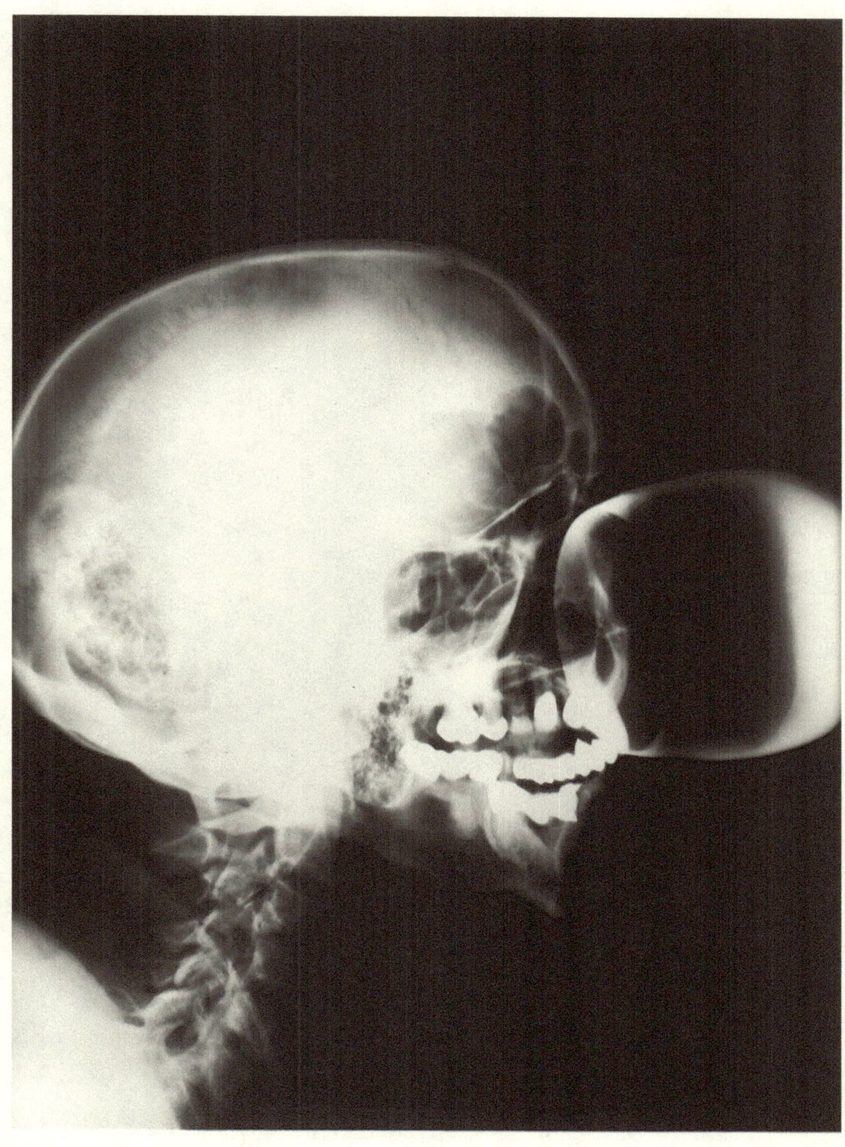

FIGURE 8.1
Isa Genzken, *X-Ray*, photo, 1991. 100 × 80 cm. Courtesy Galerie Buchholz, Cologne/Berlin/New York © VG Bild-Kunst, Bonn 2016.

NOTES

INTRODUCTION

1. Thomas Bernhard, "In Earnest," in *The Voice Imitator: 104 Stories*, trans. Kenneth J. Northcott (Chicago: University of Chicago Press, 1997), 24.

2. A preceding story, "Hotel Waldhaus," is a fine example of how even hatred is expressed with a peculiarly funny neutrality: "We had no luck with the weather and the guests at our table were repellent in every respect. They even spoiled Nietzsche for us. Even after they had had a fatal car accident and had been laid out in the church at Sils, we still hated them." (Bernhard, *The Voice Imitator*, 22.)

3. Gilles Deleuze, "The Exhausted," in *Essays Clinical and Critical*, trans. Daniel W. Smith and Michael A. Greco (Minneapolis: University of Minnesota Press, 1997), 154.

4. Gilles Deleuze, "Bartleby; or, The Formula," in *Essays Critical and Clinical*, 68. The formula *I would prefer not to*, according to Deleuze, neither rejects nor affirms a preference: "The formula is devastating because it eliminates the preferable just as mercilessly as any nonpreferred. It not only abolishes the term it refers to, and that it rejects, but also abolishes the other term it seemed to preserve and that becomes impossible. In fact, it renders them indistinct: it hollows out an ever expanding zone of indiscernibility or indetermination between some nonpreferred activities and a preferable activity." (Ibid., 71.)

5. Bernhard, *The Voice Imitator*, 25.

6. "In fact, the voice imitator did imitate voices of quite different people—all the more or less well known—from those he had imitated before the surgical society. We were allowed to express our own wishes, which the voice imitator fulfilled more readily. When, however, at the very end, we suggested that he imitate his own voice, he said he could not do that." (Bernhard, *The Voice Imitator*, 2.)

7. Julie Hecht, *Was This Man a Genius? Talks with Andy Kaufman* (New York: Simon and Schuster, 2001), 1.

8. See Florian Keller, *Andy Kaufman: Wrestling with the American Dream* (Minneapolis: University of Minnesota Press, 2005).

9. In 1980 on *The Andy Kaufman Show*, he introduces a segment called "The-Going-Too-Far-Corner."

10. Method acting arguably effaces the difference between acting and impersonation. Richard Brody, theater critic for the *New Yorker*, suggestively remarks: "There's something about modern-day acting—the style that is famously associated with Lee Strasberg's Method and that gained currency from his Actors Studio and its offshoots—that inclines towards deformations of character." And he writes of Seymour Hoffman, "Hoffman had a fury for acting and a virtuoso technique that he yoked, brilliantly, to it. He found his characters' passions within himself, took their passions upon himself, and then created, with an uncanny gift for impersonation, a set of gestures and inflections that embodied them. ... The connection of his inner life and outer skill generated a sort of emotional short circuit that overheated him terrifyingly, resulting in the justly admired intensity that he brought to every role—which was also, however, a sign of an actor giving more of himself, moment by moment, than an actor should ever be called upon, or need, to give." (Richard Brody, "Is Method Acting Destroying Actors?," February 21, 2014, www.newyorker.com.)

11. Sigmund Freud, *Letters of Sigmund Freud 1873–1939*, ed. Ernst L. Freud, trans. Tania Stern and James Stern (New York: Basic Books, 1975), 436.

12. Alex Cox, *10,000 Ways to Die: A Director's Take on the Spaghetti Western* (Harpenden, UK: Kamera, 2009).

13. Karl Marx, *Grundrisse: Foundations of a Critique of Political Economy (Rough Draft)*, trans. Marin Nicolaus (London: Penguin, 1973), 163.

14. Harold Pinter, "Samuel Beckett," in *Various Voices: Prose, Poetry, Politics* (New York: Grove Press, 1998), 55.

CHAPTER 1 THE METROLOGIST: ON MARCEL DUCHAMP'S *THREE STANDARD STOPPAGES*

1. As quoted by Linda Dalrymple Henderson, *Duchamp in Context: Science and Technology in the Large Glass and Related Works* (Princeton: Princeton University Press, 1998), 64.

2. Gilles Deleuze, "Bartleby; or, The Formula," in *Essays Clinical and Critical*, trans. Daniel W. Smith and Michael A. Greco (Minneapolis: University of Minnesota Press, 1997), 71.

3. Thierry de Duve, *Pictorial Nominalism: On Marcel Duchamp's Passage from Painting to the Readymade*, trans. Dana Polan with the author (Minneapolis: University of Minnesota Press, 1991), 173.

4. As quoted by de Duve, ibid.

5. See Henderson, *Duchamp in Context*, 63.

6. Duchamp wasn't reading Bergson but rather a book by Gleizes and Metzinger, *Du cubisme*, published in December 1912, that interpreted cubism in Bergsonian terms.

7. Protagoras's full statement runs: "Of all things the measure is man, of things that are that they are, and of the things that are not that they are not." (*The Texts of Early*

Greek Philosophy: The Complete Fragments and Selected Testimonies of the Major Presocratics, Part I, ed. and trans. Daniel W. Graham [Cambridge: Cambridge University Press, 2010], 693.) For the Greeks, the one who measures, namely the human being, is also measured by the measure. A sense that we retain, for example, when we speak of somebody being measured in their actions or their judgment.

8. In his treatment of Beckett, Deleuze speaks of exhaustion in contradistinction to being tired. To be tired is to be no longer capable of realizing something. If one is tired of going out, one does not go out, but this does not exhaust the possibility of going out. To exhaust the possibility as such is what interests Deleuze in Beckett's method. "The tired person can no longer realize, but the exhausted person can no longer possibilize" (Gilles Deleuze, "The Exhausted," in *Essays Critical and Clinical*, 152).

9. Marcel Duchamp, *Salt Seller: The Writings of Marcel Duchamp*, ed. Michel Sanouillet and Elmer Peterson (London: Thames and Hudson, 1973), 22.

10. See Alfred Jarry, *Exploits & Opinions of Dr. Faustroll, Pataphysician*, trans. Simon Watson Taylor (Boston: Exact Change, 1996), 21–22.

11. Gilles Deleuze, "An Unrecognized Precursor to Heidegger: Alfred Jarry," in *Essays Critical and Clinical*, 92.

12. Deleuze, "Bartleby; or, The Formula," 68.

13. Plato, *The Statesman*, trans. C. J. Rowe, in *Complete Works*, ed. John M. Cooper and D. S. Hutchinson (Indianapolis: Hackett, 1997), 285a.

14. Just as the "attitude of the geometer," according to Husserl, feels no need to inquire into the origin of the ideal concepts and propositions through and with which he thinks, the scientist has to rely upon the ideality of the measure without being troubled by the "art of measuring" which is practical and empirical; it must institute the ideal without having the ideal as a means to measure the difference between the real and the ideal. This act of institution must substitute a quantity for a quality which "can only be thought in gradations: the more or less straight, flat, circular, etc." (Edmund Husserl, *Crisis of the European Sciences and Transcendental Phenomenology*, trans. David Carr [Evanston: Northwestern University Press, 1970], 25.)

15. Heinrich Heine, *The Complete Poems of Heinrich Heine: A Modern English Version*, trans. Hal Draper (Boston: Suhrkamp/Insel, 1982), 99. It was Mladen Dolar who drew my attention to this poem by Heine and in particular to Freud's use of the poem. See Dolar, "Hegel and Freud," *Eflux Journal* 34 (April 2012).

16. Sigmund Freud, *The Interpretation of Dreams* (Harmondsworth, UK: Penguin, 1976), 631; as quoted in Dolar, "Hegel and Freud."

17. Louis Althusser, *Philosophy of the Encounter: Later Writings, 1978–1987*, ed. François Matheron and Oliver Corpet, trans. G. M. Goshgarian (New York: Verso, 2006), 174–175.

18. Gilles Deleuze, *Difference and Repetition*, trans. Alan Patton (New York: Columbia University Press, 1994), 29.

CHAPTER 2 THE OBJECT-SUBJECT: MARCEL BROODTHAERS, MERCHANT OF THE INSINCERE

1. Marcel Broodthaers, "Ten Thousand Francs Reward: An Interview with Irmeline Lebeer, 1974," trans. Charles Penwarden, in *Marcel Broodthaers: Collected Writings*, ed. Gloria Moure (Barcelona: Ediciones Polígrafa, 2012), 417.

2. See Benjamin H. D. Buchloh, "First and Last: Two Books by Marcel Broodthaers," in *Marcel Broodthaers: A Retrospective* (New York: Museum of Modern Art, 2016), 47 n. 3. Broodthaers included the certificate of his authentication as a work of art in the Section Littéraire of his "fictional museum," Musée d'Art Moderne, Département des Aigles.

3. Marcel Broodthaers, "Beware the Challenge!, 1963," trans. Jill Ramsey, in *Collected Writings*, 145.

4. Marcel Broodthaers, "To Be a Straight Thinker or Not to Be. To Be Blind, 1975," trans. Charles Penwarden, in *Collected Writings*, 469. Commenting as the curator of the *Museum of Modern Art, Department of Eagles*, in a letter fragment to Herbert Distel, Broodthaers writes, "As far as I am concerned, it is a question, to put it concisely, of emptying out the notion of the museum and ... the symbols (such as the eagle) that have served to establish it. In a general way, I deny artistic value as an exhaustive value based on a 'different' language, when in fact the definition of artistic activity occurs, first of all, in the field of distribution" (Broodthaers, "As Far as I Am Concerned ..., 1972," in *Collected Writings*, 331).

5. For a more elaborate account of the relationship between the readymade and the commodity form, see my "More or Less Art, More or Less a Commodity, More or Less an Object, More or Less a Subject—The Readymade and the Artist," in Nathan Brown and Petar Milat, eds., "The Art of the Concept," *Frakcija Performing Arts Journal*, no. 64–65 (2013), 62–70.

6. In the interview "Ten Thousand Francs Reward," Broodthaers says, "What reassures him is the hope that the viewer runs the risk—for a moment at least—of no longer feeling at ease" (*Collected Writings*, 416).

7. Concerning the *Section of Figures (The Eagle from the Oligocene to Today)* of the museum, Broodthaers writes, "The exhibition project is based on the identity of the Eagle as an idea and of art as an idea" (*Collected Writings*, 346). In the exhibition, Broodthaers staged a "confrontation" between the form of the museum and its spontaneous ideology, showing representations of the eagle across history in conjunction with plaques stating, "This is not a work of art."

8. Broodthaers prefers to speak of the "outmoding" of subversion. But I am alluding to his claim that "artistically, you can only find forms that reflect or critique the state of society today at this level of calmness," the "this" referring to the careful parsing of different forms of representation (*Collected Writings*, 457).

9. I am alluding to *Trébuchet (Trap)* from 1917, a series of four coat hangers attached to a board that Duchamp nailed to the floor. In conversation with Harriet Janis, Duchamp recalled "a real coat hanger that I wanted sometime to put on the wall and hang

my things on but I never did come to that—so it was on the floor and I would kick it every minute, every time I went out—I got crazy about it and I said the Hell with it, if it wants to stay there and bore me, I'll nail it down ... and then the association with the Readymade came and it was that." (As quoted in David Joselit, *Infinite Regress: Marcel Duchamp 1910–1941* [Cambridge, MA: MIT Press, 1998], 160.)

10. See Broodthaers, *Collected Writings*, 238–239.

11. Broodthaers, *Collected Writings*, 417.

12. Marcel Duchamp, *Salt Seller: The Writings of Marcel Duchamp*, ed. Michel Sanouillet and Elmer Peterson (London: Thames and Hudson, 1973), 24.

13. Ibid., 73.

14. I am of course alluding to Duchamp's pataphysical apparatus of measurement treated at length in the previous chapter: *Three Standard Stoppages*.

15. As quoted by Jacques Derrida, "An Idea of Flaubert: 'Plato's Letter,'" trans. Peter Starr, *MLN* 99, no. 4 (September 1984), 758–759 n. 9.

16. Thierry de Duve, *Kant after Duchamp* (Cambridge, MA: MIT Press, 1996), 178.

17. They attached only the following initials to the publication: P. B. T. (P for Pierre, B for Beatrice, and T for Totor, cryptically alluding to the diminutive form of Roché's nickname for Duchamp: Victor). For a detailed treatment of the "R. Mutt Case" and the important role that the *The Blindman* played in putting this event into the historical record, see de Duve's "Given the Richard Mutt Case," in *Kant after Duchamp*, 90–143. *The Blindman* not only aligns itself enthusiastically with the "sincere" cause of the exhibition, but also parodies its form: the cover of the first issue announces that the next issue "will appear as soon as YOU have sent sufficient material for it."

18. Broodthaers, *Collected Writings*, 114.

19. Interestingly Broodthaers, in the catalog accompanying *Museum of Modern Art, Department of Eagles, Section of Figures (The Eagle from the Oligocene to the Present)*, refers to the "negative inscription," this is not a work of art, as follows: "'this is not ... this is not a art work' This mean nothing other than, you dear people, how blind you are!" (*Collected Writings*, 341). One should attend to the ellipsis, which produces a hesitation, a stutter perhaps, that result in a duplication of the negation, "this is not." The duplication adds emphasis, a stress, emphasizing that this is indeed not a work of art, but the stutter also produces the effect of the not not-art. Here the "blind" spectator would be one who sheds its "eagle" eye.

20. Duchamp, *Salt Seller*, 73.

21. Ibid.

22. Broodthaers writes in an unpublished note around 1973: "Since no one form is intrinsically superior to another, the artist can use any form whatsoever—from literary expression, either written or spoken, to physical reality—in equivalent fashion" (*Collected Writings*, 367).

23. "Anartist, meaning no artist at all. That would be my conception. I don't mind being *anartist*." ("Marcel Duchamp Speaks," interview with George Heard Hamilton and Richard Hamilton, BBC Third Programme Broadcast, 1959.)

24. Duchamp's dandyism is no better expressed than in the following: "*My intention was to get away from myself, though I knew perfectly well that I was using myself. Call it a game between 'I' and 'me.'*" ("Marcel Duchamp: Interview with Katherine Kuh," in Katherine Kuh, ed., *The Artist's Voice: Talks with Seventeen Artists* [New York: Harper and Row, 1962], 83; as cited in Calvin Tomkins, *Duchamp: A Biography* [New York: Henry Holt, 1996], 160.)

25. The problem of the artist's signature is signaled in turn by Duchamp's *Signed Sign*, one of his last readymades executed for his retrospective at the Pasadena Art Museum in 1963. (See de Duve, *Kant after Duchamp*, 398–399.)

26. Broodthaers, *Collected Writings*, 452.

27. Ibid., 452–453.

28. The position of the subject trapped by Manzoni's game is that of the dandy: a figure that must appropriate the place of its own absence. Agamben has written eloquently on the matter: the "the dandy-artist must become a living corpse, constantly tending toward an *other*; a creature essentially nonhuman and antihuman. … In the abolition of any trace of subjectivity from his own person, no one has ever reached the radicalism of Beau Brummel. With an asceticism that equals the most mortifying mystical techniques, he constantly cancels from himself any trace of personality. This is the extremely serious sense of a number of his witticisms, such as "Robinson, which of the lakes do I prefer?"" (Giorgio Agamben, "The Appropriation of Unreality," in *Stanzas: Word and Phantasm in Western Culture*, trans. Ronald L. Martinez [Minneapolis: University of Minnesota Press, 1993], 50.) To be a readymade is not the consummation of life and art, but, as Broodthaers suggests, to assume a fossilized identity; it is the bone of culture.

29. Broodthaers, *Collected Writings*, 138.

30. Broodthaers writes, "I am the result of an experiment—the word is perhaps a little strong—let's say of a taste for literature, definitely; that was my starting point; however, I do believe that I am now able to express myself on the edge of things, where the world of visual arts and the world of poetry might eventually, I wouldn't say meet, but at the frontier where they part." (Broodthaers, *Collected Writings*, 410.)

31. Broodthaers's singularity "as both book-author and subject of a book prohibition" remains, as Rachel Haidu has suggested, the imprint of his authorship visible in the fingerprints "left embedded in the plaster, a reminder of the name nowhere visible on the work" (Haidu, *The Absence of Work: Marcel Broodthaers, 1964–1976* [Cambridge, MA: MIT Press, 2010], 52).

32. Broodthaers, *Collected Writings*, 456.

33. Ibid., 115.

34. Ibid., 457.

35. "Marcel Broodthaers by Marcel Broodthaers, 1965," in *Collected Writings*, 140.

36. Broodthaers, *Collected Writings*, 145.

37. Ibid.

38. Ibid.

39. Ibid.

40. Ibid., 158.

41. In a fictitious dialogue between Broodthaers and Pierre Restany, he begins: "Broodthaers is pronounced Brotars: four useless letters in the spelling of a name" (Broodthaers, *Collected Writings*, 170).

42. See Marcel Broodthaers, "I Was Studying My Character ..., 1964," in *Collected Writings*, 132.

43. "The signature of the author—painter, poet, filmmaker ... appears to me to be the beginning of a system of lies, the system that every poet, every artist tries to build in his defence ... against what exactly, I do not know." ("Interview with Marcel Broodthaers by Freddy Devree, 1971," in *Collected Writings*, 312.)

44. Broodthaers, *Collected Writings*, 456.

CHAPTER 3 A SENSE OF UMOUR: JACQUES VACHÉ

1. Gide's novel *Lafcadio's Adventures* and particularly this character's brand of dandyesque nihilism strongly impacted Vaché. As Breton writes, "From Lafcadio came a sort of 'unconscientious objection.' ... At the 'front,' Jacques Vaché (who in some respects was very hostile to Gide) dreamed of setting up his easel between French and German lines to draw Lafcadio's portrait." (André Breton, "André Gide: 1869–1951," in *Anthology of Black Humor*, trans. Mark Polizzotti [San Francisco: City Light Books, 1997], 197–198.)

2. Letter to André Breton, from X, April 29, 1917, in Jacques Vaché, "The War Letters," trans. Paul Lenti, in *4 Dada Suicides: Selected Texts of Arthur Cravan, Jacques Rigaut, Julien Torma and Jacques Vaché* (London: Atlas Press, 2005), 195.

3. Ibid.

4. Ibid.

5. Gilles Deleuze, *Difference and Repetition*, trans. Alan Patton (New York: Columbia University Press, 1994), 139.

6. Paul Lenti, "Is Suicide 'Umorous?," in *4 Dada Suicides*, 183.

7. Vaché, "The War Letters," 192.

8. Ibid., 196.

9. Letter to André Breton, from X, July 5, 1916, in Vaché, "The War Letters," 191.

10. Vaché, "The War Letters," 209 (translation modified).

11. Jacques Vaché, letter to Théodore Fraenkel, August 12, 1918: "Je rêve de bonnes Excentricités bien senties, ou de quelque bonne fourberie drôle qui fasse beaucoup de morts, le tout en costume moulé très clair, sport, voyez-moi les beaux souliers

découverts grenat?" (Vaché, *Lettres de guerre: précédées de quatre essais d'André Breton* [Paris: Eric Losfeld, 1970], 62.)

12. Vaché, "The War Letters," 210–211.

13. As quoted by Mark Polizzotti in his preface to André Breton, *The Lost Steps*, trans. Mark Polizzotti (Lincoln: University of Nebraska Press, 1996), xiii.

14. André Breton, *Anthology of Black Humor*, trans. Mark Polizzotti (San Francisco: City Light Books, 1997), 293.

15. Buster Keaton with Charles Samuels, *My Wonderful World of Slapstick* (New York: Doubleday, 1960), 13.

16. As quoted by Jana Prikryl, "The Genius of Buster Keaton," *New York Review of Books*, June 9, 2011, http://www.nybooks.com/articles/2011/06/09/genius-buster-keaton/.

17. David Hume, *The Natural History of Religion and Other Writings*, ed. Dorothy Coleman (Cambridge: Cambridge University Press, 2007), 127–128.

18. See André Breton, "The Disdainful Confession," in *Lost Steps*.

19. Ibid., 11.

CHAPTER 4 THE RIDICULOUS SUBJECT

1. André Breton, *Anthology of Black Humor*, trans. Mark Polizzotti (San Francisco: City Light Books, 1997), 211.

2. Ibid.

3. Ibid., 212.

4. André Gide, *The Counterfeiters*, trans. Dorothy Bussy (London: Penguin Books, 1931), 263.

5. Breton reports, "Another time, in a backyard, he was amusing himself by uncorking champagne with gunshots. A few bullets strayed over the fence prompting the irruption of the neighbor whose children were playing next door. 'Just imagine, if they were hit!'—'Ah!' said Jarry, 'not to worry, Madam, we'll simply make you some more.'" (*Anthology of Black Humor*, 211.)

6. Ibid., 212.

7. Breton adapts this formula for Jarry from Jarry's own formulas: "Redon: he who mysteries," or "Lautrec: he who posters" (ibid., 211).

8. Erasmus, "On Good Manners for Boys," in *The Erasmus Reader*, ed. Erika Rummel (Toronto: University of Toronto Press, 1990), 102–103.

9. Ibid., 108. The full passage reads, "Consequently, style of dress should be in accordance with, one's means and station, one's locality and its standards, neither conspicuous by its shabbiness nor indicative of opulence, loose living, or arrogance. A degree of negligence in dress suits young men provided it does not lapse into slovenliness. Disgustingly some people decorate the hems of their shirts and tunics with drops of urine or encrust their shirt-fronts and sleeves with a repulsive splattering, not unfortunately of plaster, but of snot and phlegm" (108–109).

10. Heinrich von Kleist, "On the Marionette Theater," trans. Thomas G. Neumiller, *The Drama Review* (TDR) 16, no. 3, The Puppet Issue (September 1972), 24.

11. "From that day on, from that very moment on, an inexplicable change took place in this young man. He began to stand in front of the mirror all day long, and one virtue after another dropped away from him. An invisible and inexplicable power like an iron net seemed to seize upon the spontaneity of his bearing, and after a year there was no trace of the charm that had so delighted those who knew him. There is only one other person alive today who witnessed that strange and unhappy incident, and who would confirm it for you word for word as I have related it." (Ibid., 25.)

12. Charles Baudelaire, "On the Essence of Laughter," in *The Painter of Modern Life and Other Essays*, trans. and ed. Jonathan Mayne (London: Phaidon Press, 1964), 152.

13. Charles Baudelaire, "The Bad Glazier," in *Paris Spleen*, trans. Louise Varère (New York: New Directions, 1947), 12.

14. Ibid.

15. Jean-Paul Sartre, *Baudelaire*, trans. Martin Turnell (New York: New Directions, 1950), 27.

16. Ibid., 32.

17. Ibid., 33.

18. Ibid., 22.

19. Ibid., 27–28.

20. Baudelaire, "On the Essence of Laughter," 161.

21. Ibid., 165.

22. Ibid.,156.

23. Ibid., 154.

24. Ibid., 156.

25. Ibid., 154.

26. Giorgio Agamben, *Stanzas: Word and Phantasm in Western Culture*, trans. Ronald L. Martinez (Minneapolis: University of Minnesota Press, 1993), 33.

27. Freud, "Fetishism," in *The Standard Edition of the Complete Psychological Works of Sigmund Freud*, vol. 21, trans. and ed. James Strachey (London: Hogarth Press, 1961), 154.

28. Baudelaire, "On the Essence of Laughter," 164.

29. Ibid., 158.

30. Ibid., 157.

31. Ibid., 161.

32. It is worth recalling that Gide introduces Jarry into *The Counterfeiters* by having a character ask: "'Who is that pierrot?' … 'It's Alfred Jarry, the author of *Ubu Roi*'" (262).

33. In *Discourse, Figure*, Lyotard writes, "When you produce a verb with a noun, an event happens: the system of the rules of language [*langue*] not only is unable to

account for this novel use, but opposes it, resists it; the relation that arises between it and the statement is one of conflict." (Jean-François Lyotard, *Discourse, Figure*, trans. Antony Hudek and Mary Lydon [Minneapolis: University of Minnesota Press, 2011], 141.)

CHAPTER 5 COUNTING FOR NOTHING: THE NIHILIST

1. Paul Valéry, *Monsieur Teste*, trans. Jackson Mathews (New York: A. A. Knopf, 1947), 88–89.

2. See Friedrich Nietzsche, *The Birth of Tragedy and Other Writings*, ed. Ronald Geuss and Ronald Speiers, trans. Ronald Speiers (Cambridge: Cambridge University Press, 1999), 23.

3. This nihilism stems from the pathos of disappointment, of thwarted expectation, of meaning lost, which lies at the root for Nietzsche of all *passive* nihilism. See Friedrich Nietzsche, *The Will to Power*, ed. Walter Kaufmann, trans. Walter Kaufmann and R. J. Hollingdale (New York: Vintage Books, 1967), 12.

4. The name Monsieur Teste, whose first name, Edmond, is hardly mentioned, is, of course, of tremendous significance for a subject who himself is a nominalist. "Teste" alludes both to the old French for head (tête in modern French) and also the Latin *testis*, which refers to a witness or a spectator in the sense of testament. *Testis* is also the word for testicle.

5. Jacques Lacan, "Science and Truth," in *Écrits*, trans. Bruce Fink (New York: W. W. Norton, 2006), 731.

6. Jackson Mathews, "A Note on Valéry," in *Monsieur Teste*, xii.

7. As quoted by Mathews, ibid.

8. The simile is extracted from Valéry's late autobiographical poem "Station of the Terrace," trans. Brian Stimpson, included as an appendix to Anne M. Mairesse, "Return to Monsieur Teste?, or 'What Is a Man Capable of?': Valéry, Anthropologist of Modernity," *MLN* 117 (2002), 1023.

9. Immanuel Kant, *Anthropology from a Pragmatic Point of View*, trans. Robert B. Louden (Cambridge: Cambridge University Press, 2006), 127. (The reference numbers in this edition refer to the page numbering of the original German edition.)

10. Jacques Lacan, *Seminar XI: The Four Fundamental Concepts of Psychoanalysis*, ed. Jacques-Alain Miller, trans. Alan Sheridan (New York: W. W. Norton, 1978), 20 (translation modified).

11. Valéry, *Monsieur Teste*, 90.

12. Friedrich Nietzsche, *The Gay Science*, ed. Bernard Williams, trans. Josefine Nauckhoff (Cambridge: Cambridge University Press, 2001), 204.

13. "Man is different from me, from you. That which thinks is never that which it thinks about, and since the first is a form with a voice, the second takes all forms and all voices. So, no one is man, M. Teste least of all." (Valéry, *Monsieur Teste*, 71.)

14. In the *Gay Science*, Nietzsche writes, "Faith is always most desired and most urgently needed where will is lacking" (*The Gay Science*, 205).

15. Nietzsche, *The Will to Power*, 14.

16. Ibid., 17.

17. Nietzsche, *The Gay Science*, 347.

18. Fyodor Dostoevsky, *Demons*, trans. Richard Pevear and Larissa Volokhonsy (London: Everyman, 2000), 419. See Shane Weller, *Modernism and Nihilism* (New York: Palgrave Macmillan, 2011), 29.

19. Friedrich Nietzsche, *Beyond Good and Evil*, ed. Rolf-Peter Horstmann and Judith Norman, trans. Judith Norman (Cambridge: Cambridge University Press, 2002), 11.

20. This tendency accounts for the most virulent strain of the Dada and surrealist interest in primitivism, animating Georges Bataille and Michel Leiris, Arthur Cravan and the Baroness Elsa von Freytag-Loringhoven; Cravan's statements are exemplary in their extremity: "Je mangerais ma merde [I would eat my shit]" and "Glory is a scandal. Let me state once and for all: I do not wish to be civilized" (as quoted by Roger Conover in his introduction to selections from Arthur Cravan, in *4 Dada Suicides: Selected Texts of Arthur Cravan, Jacques Rigaut, Julien Torma and Jacques Vaché* [London: Atlas Press, 2005], 23–24).

21. This is a metaphor that Nietzsche uses to speak of that most fundamental of disorientating events: the death of God. "Aren't we straying as though through an infinite nothing? Isn't empty space breathing at us?" (Nietzsche, *The Gay Science*, 120).

22. G. W. F. Hegel, *Phenomenology of Spirit*, trans. A. V. Miller (Oxford: Oxford University Press, 1977), §339.

23. Ibid., §333.

24. As quoted in Domna C. Stanton, *The Aristocrat as Art: A Study of the Honnête Homme and the Dandy in Seventeenth- and Nineteenth-Century Literature* (New York: Columbia University Press, 1980), 100–101.

25. Denis Diderot, *Rameau's Nephew and First Satire*, trans. Margaret Mauldon (Oxford: Oxford University Press, 2006), 3.

26. I am here alluding to the following passage: "[The true spirit of culture] exists in the universal talk and destructive judgment which strips of their significance all those moments which are supposed to count as the true being and as actual members of the whole, and is equally this nihilistic game which it plays with itself" (Hegel, *Phenomenology of Spirit*, §521).

27. Diderot, *Rameau's Nephew*, 3–4.

28. Giorgio Agamben, *The Man without Content*, trans. Georgia Albert (Stanford: Stanford University Press, 1999), 56–57.

29. Pierre Klossowski, *Nietzsche and the Vicious Circle*, trans. Daniel W. Smith (Chicago: University of Chicago Press, 1997), xv.

30. "In him I sensed feelings that made me shudder, a terrible obstinacy in delirious experience. He was a being absorbed in his own variation, one who becomes his own system, who gives himself up wholly to the frightful discipline of the free mind, and who sets his joys to killing one another, the stronger killing the weaker." (Valéry, *Monsieur Teste*, 13.)

31. Miller writes, "Suture names the relation of the subject to the chain of its discourse; we shall see that it figures there as the element which is lacking, in the form of a stand-in [*tenant-lieu*]. For, while there lacking, it is not purely and simply absent. Suture, by extension—the general relation of lack to the structure of which it is an element, inasmuch as it implies the position of a taking-the-place-of." (Jacques-Alain Miller, "Suture (Elements of the Logic of the Signifier)," trans. Jacqueline Rose, in *Screen* 18, no. 4 [Winter 1977–1978], 25–26.) See also *Concept and Form*, vol. 1: *Key Texts from the Cahiers pour l'Analyse*, ed. Peter Hallward and Knox Peden (London: Verso, 2012).

32. Edgar Allan Poe, *The Complete Stories* (New York: Alfred A. Knopf, 1993), 418. In quoting this passage, Clément Rosset emphasizes that the uncanny double appears as an index of a reality of which the subject is deprived. It is not the double that is an unreal specter; the double, on the contrary, awakens this uncanny feeling in oneself: "it isn't the other who is my double, but I who am the other's double. His is the reality, mine the shadow" (Rosset, *The Real and Its Double*, trans. Chris Turner [London: Seagull Books, 2012], 56).

33. Valéry, *Monsieur Teste*, 93–94.

34. Ibid., 88.

35. Nietzsche, *The Will to Power*, 318.

36. Valéry, *Monsieur Teste*, 94.

37. Ibid., 93.

38. Jean Améry, *On Suicide: A Discourse on Voluntary Death* (Bloomington: Indiana University Press, 1999), 19.

39. Valéry, *Monsieur Teste*, 91.

40. Ibid., 86.

41. Such a support brings to mind Democritus's conceptual coinage: *den*. The Greek for *nothing*, μηδέν (*mêden*), is formed from a negation (*mê*) of that which is one, ἕν (*hen*): *mê'hen*. *Mêden* names that which is not something, which is to say, *not a one*. Barbara Cassin writes: "The etymology is obvious: the Plato of the *Sophist*, for example, makes it clear to drive home the point about performative self-contradiction; when one says *mêden*, 'nothing,' one says *mê ti* [μή τι], 'not something,' that is, *hen ge ti* [ἕν γε τι], 'something one' (237e1–2 and 237d7); *mêden* thus means *mêd'hen*, 'not even one.' However, unlike *to mê on*, here we have a single word, and not a composite expression: *mêden*, like *ouden*, in a single word, is the neuter pronoun we find even in Homer. With *mêden*, negation becomes an affirmed, even a positive entity, like 'nothing' or 'no one.'" (Barbara Cassin, "Esti," in *Dictionary of Untranslatable: A Philosophical Lexicon*, ed. Barbara Cassin, trans. ed. Emily Apter, Jacques Lezra, and Michael Wood [Princeton:

Princeton University Press, 2014], 320.) Democritus's *den* can be translated as "hing." To quote Cassin again: "*Den* can be thought only after the one, as a subtractive operation and not as a provenance, truncated or not. It cannot be submitted to dialectics precisely by not being a negation of negation, taken up and sublated, but a subtraction on the basis of negation, and thus a surplus, a fiction obtained by critical secondarity. It is not an entry but an exit, a way out which makes the origin stumble and deviates the history of philosophy, hence also the history of physics, just as the *clinamen* to which Lacan has compared it." (Alain Badiou and Barbara Cassin, *Il n'y pas de rapport sexuel* [Paris: Fayard, 2010], 83–84.) As quoted by Mladen Dolar in his incisive essay "Tyche, clinamen, den," *Continental Philosophy Review* 46 (2013): 223–239, that forges an original ontological position—ex-centric to Deleuze's or Badiou's diverging embrace of atomism—by traversing Lacan's thinking of *tyche* and *automaton*, *clinamen*, and *den*. With the *den* we touch upon thought's senseless and aleatory exigency as that fiction that makes a difference, differentiating the void from the void.

CHAPTER 6 SLIPPERED NEGLIGENCE: THE DANDY

1. Oswald Wiener, "Remarks on Some Tendencies of the 'Vienna Group,'" trans. David Britt, *October* 97 (Summer 2001), 128–129.

2. Throughout the chapter I refer to the dandy as an "it," using "he" or "she" only when referring to a specific dandy who happens to be male or female, for example Beau Brummel or the Marquise de Mertuil. The use of this impersonal pronoun when referring to the dandy as such is decisive, since the dandy's impersonality is of capital importance. Historically speaking, dandies have been men; however, androgyny has always been an important ingredient of the dandy's dissolute identity.

3. William Hazlitt, "Brummelliana," in *Selected Writings*, ed. John Cook (Oxford: Oxford University Press, 1991), 159.

4. Charles Baudelaire, "The Painter of Modern Life," in *The Painter of Modern Life and Other Essays*, trans. and ed. Jonathan Mayne (London: Phaidon Press, 1964), 28–29.

5. The character of des Esseintes is largely modeled on the French aristocrat Robert de Montesquiou, who would also inspire Proust's Baron de Charlus in *The Remembrance of Things Past*, a dandy-decadent who pushed his eccentricities to a ridiculous extreme. Mallarmé, who dedicates the poem "Prose" to des Esseintes which begins "Hyberbole!," once visited Montesquiou's home, and it is likely, as Robert Baldick suggests, that Huysmans heard about the manner in which Montesquiou furnished his home from Mallarmé himself. See Robert Baldick, *The Life of J.-K. Huysmans*, ed. Brendan King (1955; Sawtry, UK: Dedalus, 2006), 122–123.

6. Hazlitt, "Brummelliana," 159.

7. In *From Thirty Years with Freud*, Theodor Reik writes, "Freud once varied the saying '*Le style, c'est l'homme*' to '*Le style, c'est l'histoire de l'homme*.'" As quoted in Philippe Lacoue-Labarthe, "The Echo of the Subject," in *Typographies: Mimesis, Philosophy, Politics*, ed. Christopher Fynsk (Cambridge, MA: Harvard University Press, 1989), 166.

8. Charles Baudelaire, *My Heart Laid Bare*, trans. Ariana Reines (Mal-O-Mar, 2009), 5.

9. Paul Valéry, *Monsieur Teste*, trans. Jackson Mathews (New York: A. A. Knopf, 1947), 85–86.

10. Ibid., 14.

11. Oswald Wiener, "Eine Art Einzige," in *Riten der Selbstauflösung*, ed. Verena von der Heyden-Rynsch (Munich: Matthes & Seitz Verlag, 1982), 52. It should be noted that Wiener himself writes in what one could call a *parasyntactic* style and, like his fellow member of the Vienna Group, Konrad Bayer, writes in all lower-case letters, not capitalizing either the first letter of a sentence or nouns (as is conventional in German). An unauthorized translation of the first section of this essay, "Du Dandysme . . . ," by Jeffrey D. Gower and the late Ludwig Fischer, appeared in *Machete*, May 2011. For the archive of *Machete* see the website of the gallery Marginal Utility: www.marginalutility.org

12. Wiener, "Eine Art Einzige," 52 n. 20.

13. Ibid., 36.

14. Ibid.

15. Ibid., 54. Baudelaire is already clear on the matter: see "The Painter of Modern Life," 28.

16. Oswald Wiener, "Nachbemerkung," in *Riten der Selbstauflösung*, 325.

17. I am here transposing Wiener's language into my own, shifting idioms by bringing his own discourse into relation with structuralist forms of thought as they are developed, for example, in Deleuze's essay "How Do We Recognize Structuralism?" Although my own account does not deviate radically, in my view, from Wiener's own, I do not feel hermeneutically beholden to the idiom of his discourse. Wiener's own interest in formal systems, although by no means exclusive of structuralism so defined, tends to be concerned more with systems theory, cybernetics, and artificial intelligence. He is, for example, the German translator of Herbert A. Simon's *The Sciences of the Artificial* (Cambridge, MA: MIT Press, 1996). He does, however, provide the following as an instructive example of dandyesque application: "Freedom of interpretation—a fabulous example of dandyesque audacity is Roman Jakobson's and Claude Lévi-Strauss's interpretation of *Chats*; everything that these authors know about Baudelaire—I presume—that can be wondered about him, is liquidated [*ausgerottet*]; an icy glance sees a possibility, a severe mind [*scharfer geist*] drives it along" (Wiener, "Eine Art Einzige," 55).

18. Michel Foucault touches on this point in his essay "What Is Enlightenment?": "Modern man, for Baudelaire, is not the man who goes off to discover himself, his secrets and his hidden truth; he is the man who tries to invent himself. This modernity does not 'liberate man in his own being'; it compels him to face the task of producing himself." (*The Essential Works of Michel Foucault 1954–1984*, vol. 1: *Ethics: Subjectivity and Truth*, ed. Paul Rabinow, trans. Robert Hurley et al. [New York: New Press, 1997], 312.)

19. Wiener, "Eine Art Einzige," 40–41.

20. Julien Torma, "Euphorisms," in 4 *Dada Suicides: Selected Texts of Arthur Cravan, Jacques Rigaut, Julien Torma and Jacques Vaché* (London: Atlas Press, 2005), 153–154.

21. Oswald Wiener, "some remarks on konrad bayer," in Peter Weibel, ed., *The Vienna Group: A Moment of Modernity 1954–60* (Berlin: Springer, 1997), 42.

22. Wiener, "Eine Art Einzige," 37.

23. Baudelaire, "The Painter of Modern Life," 28.

24. Kant distinguishes the transcendental subject from psychological personality: "Yet we can lay at the basis of this science nothing but the simple, and by itself quite empty, presentation I, of which we cannot even say that it is a concept, but only that it is a mere consciousness accompanying all concepts. Now through this I or *he* or it (the thing) that thinks, nothing more is presented than a transcendental subject of thoughts = x." (Immanuel Kant, *Critique of Pure Reason*, trans. Werner S. Pluhar [Indianapolis: Hackett, 1996], 385.) The notion of a spiritual automaton (*automa spirituale*) derives from Spinoza's use of this concept in the *Treatise on the Emendation of the Intellect*: "This is the same as what the ancients said, i.e., that true knowledge proceeds from cause to effect—except that as far as I know they never conceived the soul [*psyche*] (as we do here) as acting according to certain laws, like a *spiritual automaton*." (Benedictus de Spinoza, *The Collected Works of Spinoza* [Princeton: Princeton University Press, 1985], 37.)

25. Wiener, "Eine Art Einzige," 36.

26. Valéry, *Monsieur Teste*, 19.

27. Arthur Rimbaud, "Letter to George Izambard, Charleville, May 13, 1871," in *Rimbaud Complete*, vol. 1, *Poetry and Prose*, ed. and trans. Wyatt Mason (New York: Modern Library, 2002), 365. The translation has been modified.

28. Wiener, "Eine Art Einzige," 38.

29. Ibid., 59.

30. Inhabiting an inverted world where falsity is truth, where anchors are made out of cork, Huysmans makes a "vulgar equation," as Wiener puts it, between sickness and artificiality: "krank = künstlich" (ibid.).

31. Ibid.

32. Valéry, *Monsieur Teste*, 14.

33. Wiener, "Eine Art Einzige," 59.

34. Valéry, *Monsieur Teste*, 22. As the narrator describes, "This man had early known the importance of what might be called human plasticity. He had tried to find out its limits and its laws. How deeply he must have thought about his own malleability!" (Ibid., 13.)

35. Ibid., 14.

36. This is perhaps the reason for Wiener's addition at the end of his essay of discussion of Hadaly's and Parry's "proofing" of the Turing test.

37. Valéry, *Monsieur Teste*, 14.

38. Ibid.

39. Wiener, "Eine Art Einzige," 60.

40. Ibid.

41. Valéry, *Monsieur Teste*, 20.

42. Ibid.

43. Ibid.

44. Ibid., 85.

45. Ibid., 44.

46. See *Cracking Up*, dir. Jerry Lewis, 1983.

47. Hazlitt, "Brummelliana," *Selected Writings*, 161.

48. Virginia Woolf, *Beau Brummel* (New York: Remington and Hooper, 1930), 7.

49. Ellen Moers's writes: "To the dandy the self is not an animal, but a gentleman. Instinctual reactions, passions and enthusiasms are animal, and thus abominable. Here the dandy temperament diverges most widely from the romantic, which dominated the major literature of Brummel's time." (Moers, *The Dandy: Brummel to Beerbohm* [London: Secker and Warburg, 1960], 18.)

50. William Shakespeare, *Timon of Athens*, 4.3.54–56.

51. Ibid., 5.1.520–525.

52. Ibid., 3.1.41.

53. Moers writes, "The dandy has no occupation, and no obvious source of support. Money does not strike him as a subject worthy of his attention" (Moers, *The Dandy*, 18).

CHAPTER 7 THE HAPPY MELANCHOLIC

1. "The books we need are of the kind that act upon us like a misfortune, that make us suffer like the death of someone we love more than ourselves, that make us feel as if we were on the verge of suicide or lost in a forest remote from all human adaptation. A book should serve as the axe for the frozen sea within us." (Franz Kafka, *Letters to Friends, Family, and Editors* [New York: Schocken Books, 1977], 16.)

2. László Krasznahorkai, *War and War*, trans. George Szirtes (New York: New Directions, 2006).

3. As quoted by Clément Rosset, *Joyful Cruelty: Toward a Philosophy of the Real*, ed. and trans. David F. Bell (New York: Oxford University Press, 1993), 76.

4. "Cruor, from which *crudelis* (cruel) as well *crudus* (not digested, indigestible) are derived, designates torn and bloody flesh, that is, the thing itself stripped of all its ornaments and ordinary external accoutrements, in this case skin, and thus reduced to its unique reality, as bloody as it is indigestible. Thus reality is cruel—and indigestible—as soon as one removes from it everything which is not reality in order to consider it in itself." (Ibid.)

5. See Walter Benjamin's suggestive reading of Dürer's *Melencolia I* offered in *The Origin of German Tragic Drama*, trans. John Osborne (New York: Verso, 1998) which draws on and radicalizes the scholarly work of Saxl and Panofsky.

6. Walter Benjamin, "Central Park," in *The Writer of Modern Life: Essays on Charles Baudelaire*, ed. Michael W. Jennings, trans. Howard Eiland, Edmund Jephcott, Rodney Livingston, and Harry Zohn (Cambridge, MA: Belknap Press of Harvard University Press, 2006), 138.

7. This fantasy is belied by the volcano spitting forth Empedocles' bronzed sandal.

8. Julia Kristeva, *Black Sun: Depression and Melancholia*, trans. Leon S. Roudiez (New York: Columbia University Press, 1989), 72–73.

9. F. Scott Fitzgerald, "The Crack-Up," in *On Booze* (New York: New Directions, 1945), 11.

10. Ibid., 15.

11. Ibid., 29.

12. Ibid., 32.

13. Gilles Deleuze, *The Logic of Sense*, trans. Mark Lester, ed. Constantin V. Boundas (New York: Columbia University Press, 1990), 158.

14. Giorgio Agamben, *Stanzas: Word and Phantasm in Western Culture*, trans. Ronald L. Martinez (Minneapolis: University of Minnesota Press, 1993), 26.

15. The epigraphs run as follows. Rilke: "Now loss, cruel as it may be, cannot do anything against possession: it completes it, if you wish, it affirms it. It is not, at bottom, but a second acquisition—this time wholly internal—and equally intense." Hölderlin: "Many attempted in vain to say the most joyful things joyfully; here, finally, they are expressed in mourning." (Agamben, *Stanzas*, 1.)

16. Sigmund Freud, "Mourning and Melancholia," in *General Psychological Theory: Papers on Metapsychology*, ed. Philip Rieff (New York: Simon and Schuster, 1991), 163.

17. Ibid., 168.

18. Ibid., 164.

19. Ibid.

20. Agamben, *Stanzas*, 20.

21. Ibid.

22. Ibid., 25.

23. Ibid.

24. Freud, "Mourning and Melancholia," 168.

25. Agamben, *Stanzas*, 21.

26. Kristeva, *Black Sun*, 47.

27. Kristeva writes, "depressed [or melancholic] persons do not forget how to use signs. They keep them, but the signs seem absurd, delayed, ready to be extinguished,

because of the splitting that affects them. For instead of bonding the affect caused by loss [as is the case in mourning], the depressed sign disowns the affect as well as the signifier, thus admitting that the depressed subject has remained prisoner of the nonlost object (the Thing)." (Kristeva, *Black Sun*, 47.)

28. Benjamin, "Central Park," 147.

29. Benjamin's full statement runs as follows: "The Baudelairian allegory—unlike the Baroque allegory—bears traces of the rage needed to break into the world, to lay waste its harmonious structures" ("Central Park," 149).

30. Robert Burton, *The Anatomy of Melancholy*, ed. Holbrook Jackson (New York: New York Review of Books, 2001), 250.

31. Benjamin, "Central Park," 137.

32. Charles Baudelaire, "Spleen (II)," in *Flowers of Evil*, trans. Richard Howard (Boston: David R. Godine, 1982), 75.

33. Charles Baudelaire, "The Stranger," in *Paris Spleen*, trans. Louise Varère (New York: New Directions, 1947), 1.

34. Charles Baudelaire, "Sympathetic Horror," in *Flowers of Evil*, 79.

35. "The condition of success of this sacrificial task is that the artist should take to its extreme consequences the principle of loss and self-dispossession. Rimbaud's programmatic exclamation 'I is an other' (*je est un autre*) must be taken literally: the redemption of objects is impossible except by virtue of becoming an object. As the work of art must destroy and alienate itself to become an absolute commodity, so the dandy-artist must become a living corpse, constantly tending toward an *other*, a creature essentially nonhuman and antihuman." (Agamben, *Stanzas*, 50.)

36. Charles Baudelaire, "The Cracked Bell," in *Flowers of Evil*, 74.

37. Charles Baudelaire, "The Happy Corpse," in *Flowers of Evil*, 72–73.

38. Benjamin, "Central Park," 138.

39. "Baroque allegory sees the corpse only from the outside. Baudelaire sees it from within." (Ibid., 163.)

CONCLUSION: A HOLE IN A THING IT IS NOT

1. Ralph Waldo Emerson, "Prudence," in *Essays and Lectures* (New York: Library of America, 1983), 365.

2. Herman Melville writes this in an 1862 marginal note referring to the passage of Emerson's "Prudence" quoted above. See Stephen Matterson's "Introduction" to Melville's *The Confidence-man: His Masquerade* (New York: Penguin Books, 1990), xxi.

3. The idea for this chapter had its accidental beginning in a conversation with Daniel Buchholz and Cheyney Thompson in a bar called the Rum Trader, Berlin, after the opening of the latter's exhibition "Chambered Shells and Birdwings," September 19–October 31, 2015.

4. Jacques Lacan, *Seminar XI: The Four Fundamental Concepts of Psychoanalysis*, ed. Jacques-Alain Miller, trans. Alan Sheridan (New York: W. W. Norton, 1978), 61.

5. Ibid.

6. In a statement delivered at a symposium at Windham College in 1968: "I would say a thing is a hole in a thing it is not. Our whole education is conducted by linguistic means. Language is mostly devoted to symbols, and art has very little to do with that. Any artist can symbolize but very few artists can execute. I would say all ideas are the same except in execution. They lie in the head. In terms of the artist, the only difference between one idea and another is how it is executed." Carl Andre, *Cuts: Texts 1959–2004*, ed. James Meyer (Cambridge, MA: MIT Press, 2005), 84.

7. Dalia Judovitz writes, "*Drain Stopper* is an item of hardware that Duchamp recycles from his bathroom in Spain, modified by being thickened with additional lead. *Marcel Duchamp Art Medal* is a cast from *Drain Stopper* in several versions, including bronze, steel, and silver editions, issued by the International Numismatic Agency (also known as the International Collectors Society, New York). ... Thus, like *Fountain*, *Drain Stopper* is only provisionally a work of art; it is more like a stopper—a stopgap measure or makeshift substitute (a pun on *bouche-trou*, its French title)—or a punctuation mark (indicating a pause or delay), rather than an actual art object. Poised between the wet (an allusion to painting as a purely material art 'the splashing of paint') and the dry (a conceptual interpretation of art that includes mechanical reproduction), *Drain Stopper* acts like a regulative device controlling the transition between art and nonart. Like a pun, 'stopper'—which means to regulate sound (as pitch in music) or light (as a photographic aperture)—mechanically triggers both the linguistic and the visual registers." Judovitz, *Unpacking Duchamp: Art in Transit* (Berkeley: University of California Press, 1995), 186–188.

8. Julien Torma, "Euphorisms," in *4 Dada Suicides: Selected Texts of Arthur Cravan, Jacques Rigaut, Julien Torma and Jacques Vaché* (London: Atlas Press, 2005), 135–136.

9. As quoted by Jean-Michel Rabaté, *Think, Pig! Beckett at the Limit of the Human* (New York: Fordham University Press, 2016), 6.

10. Friedrich Nietzsche, *Writings from the Late Notebooks*, ed. Rüdiger Bittner, trans. Kate Sturge (Cambridge: Cambridge University Press, 2003), 117.

11. Ibid.

INDEX

www.ingramcontent.com/pod-product-compliance
Lightning Source LLC
LaVergne TN
LVHW051004080826
845145LV00009B/2443

* 9 7 8 0 2 6 2 5 3 4 1 9 2 *